NATIVE AMERICAN ASTROLOGY

The Wisdom of the Four Winds

NATIVE AMERICAN ASTROLOGY

The Wisdom of the Four Winds

WINFRIED NOÉ

Sterling Publishing Co., Inc.
New York

Translated from the German by Elisabeth Reinersmann
English translation edited by Jeanette Green
Designed by Judy Morgan & Illustrated by Saniela Schneider

Library of Congress Cataloging-in-Publication Data Available

3   5   7   9   10   8   6   4   2

Published by Sterling Publishing Company, Inc.
387 Park Avenue South, New York, N.Y. 10016
Originally published and © 1997 by Falken Verlag
(Falken TaschenBuch) under the title
Das Indianische Horoskop: Astrologie und Weisheit der Vier Winde
English translation © 1998 by Sterling Publishing Co., Inc.
Distributed in Canada by Sterling Publishing
C/o Canadian Manda Group, One Atlantic Avenue, Suite 105
Toronto, Ontario, Canada M6K 3E7
Distributed in Great Britain and Europe by Cassell PLC
Wellington Houst, 125 Strand, London WC2R 0BB, England
Distributed in Australia by Capricorn Link (Australia) Pty Ltd.
P.O. Box 6651 Baulkham Hills, Business Centre, NSW 2153, Australia

Sterling ISBN 0-8069-4234-7

CONTENTS

▼▼▼▼▼▼▼▼▼▼▼▼▼▼▼▼▼▼▼▼▼▼▼▼▼▼▼▼

▼▼▼ ▼ ▼▼ ▼▼▼▼ ▼▼▼▼ ▼▼▼ ▼▼▼ ▼ ▼▼

▼▼▼▼▼▼▼▼▼▼▼▼▼▼▼▼▼▼▼▼▼▼▼▼▼▼▼▼▼▼▼

THE CYCLE OF NATURE

NATIVE AMERICAN COSMOLOGY

‡‡‡

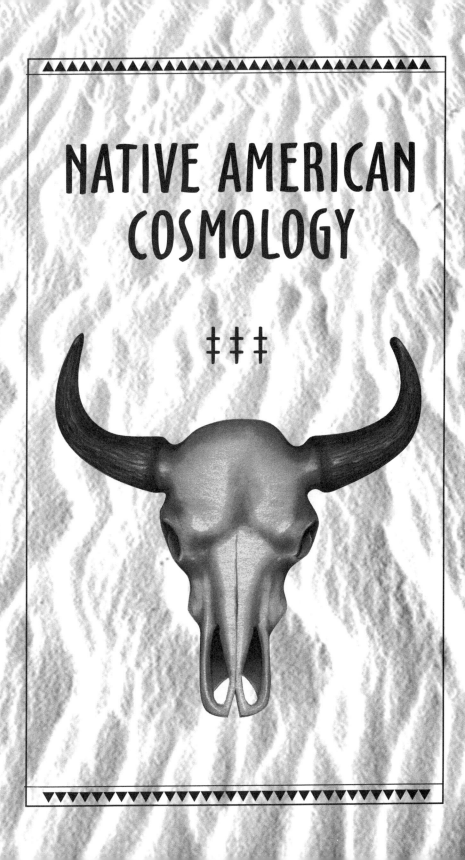

Grandfather Sun and Grandmother Moon

Someone once said: "Europeans are crazy because they think with the head, and not the heart." This also describes the basic difference between the way Westerners and Native Americans, the First Peoples of North and South America, view the world.

Native Americans have traditionally spoken of Mother Earth and Father Heaven, Grandmother Moon and Grandfather Sun as ancestors from whom they trace their very being. Native Americans understand their place in the material and spiritual worlds. Unlike many other peoples in the Western world, they feel reverence, respect, and love for Earth, the Great Mother. Who could mistreat, exploit, and poison one's own mother? From ancient times, Native Americans have tried to live in harmony with the elements and forces of nature. Western people, in contrast, often use nature shortsightedly, carelessly, and egotistically to satisfy immediate needs for security and comfort. For the collective well-being, all of us should heed the message of the Native American people and begin thinking less with our egos and appetites and more with our hearts.

The Cycle of Nature

Observation of the cycle of nature informs Native American cosmology, much as it does traditional Western astrology. The differences between the two systems are few, but Native American cosmology is more connected with nature and the animals that inhabit the Earth rather than the observed changes of stars in the heavens. The cycle of nature, which follows the Sun's apparent movement around the Earth, phases of the Moon, the growth of plants, and the character and behavior of important creatures of the Earth, is central to traditional Native Americans' way of being.

What Westerners would call the "zodiac," Native Americans call the Earth or Medicine Wheel. Since Native Americans closely observe changes in nature, their cosmology is Earth-centered. They view the seasons of nature as mirroring the mystery of eternal life and constant renewal.

The Native American Medicine Wheel, identified with the Earth, depends on harmony with nature. The Native American term *medicine* (really our mistranslation of a native word) is not used for healing, but instead, empowerment. It helps make a person whole, healthy, and complete. Medicine, the stuff of the Earth, can also be a meaningful object—a memento, feather, or stone. It can also be an act, idea, vision, or dream (inspiration from the very source of our being) which can help someone regain his center, become whole.

Native American animal spirits, which animate their cosmology, or zodiac, also contain valuable medicine: each animal totem or sign specifies a stage of development in the cycle of nature or the rhythm of life. These spirits provide people with valuable hints about where they are in the great journey of life and of what they should be mindful.

The Animal Totem

The Native American *totem* means emblem, or sign. We often see animal likenesses in Native American carvings and jewelry. These totem animals, most notable in the Northwest Pacific region, can be identified as character or personality types, or spirits, which also people the fetishes, folk tales, mythology, cosmology, lore, and masking traditions of many Native American nations. These animal spirits dominate artifacts in North America. Each of the twelve Moons, or Moon phases, has an associated animal, which may be considered a birth totem or birth sign. Native Americans feel a close affinity with animals and all of nature. And indeed, animals seem to display some of the character types that make up Native American totems, which are akin to Western astrology. The table on page 12 gives the Native American totem animal, its symbol (our graphic representation), and its dates or Moon phase with its corresponding sign from Western astrology.

NATIVE AMERICAN TOTEMS

Falcon	March 21–April 19	(Aries)
Beaver	April 20–May 20	(Taurus)
Deer	May 21–June 20	(Gemini)
Woodpecker	June 21–July 21	(Cancer)
Salmon	July 22–August 21	(Leo)
Brown Bear	August 22–September 21	(Virgo)
Raven	September 22–October 22	(Libra)
Serpent	October 23–November 22	(Scorpio)
Owl	November 23–December 21	(Sagittarius)
Goose	December 22–January 19	(Capricorn)
Otter	January 20–February 18	(Aquarius)
Wolf	February 19–March 20	(Pisces)

The Elements

Four basic elements—earth, air, fire, and water—from traditional astrology are said to form life since they are conceived as vital energies that inform all things. Since each person is influenced by the element under which he is born, he should attempt to live in harmony with it. While the elements really speak for themselves—provided one is aware of them—we define them here.

‡ **Earth** stands for corporality, focus, stability, structure, and orderliness.

‡ **Air** represents intellect, thought, interest, movement, and flexibility.

‡ **Fire** indicates spirit, creativity, intention, and action.

‡ **Water** contains soulfulness, emotions, receptivity, devotion, silence, and empathy.

Clans and Elements

Each of the four elements—earth, air, fire, and water—has been assigned to four important clans, each of which has three animal totems.

> **Earth (Tortoise clan):** Beaver, Brown Bear, and Goose
> **Air (Butterfly clan):** Deer, Raven, and Otter
> **Fire (Hawk clan):** Falcon, Salmon, and Owl
> **Water (Frog clan):** Woodpecker, Serpent, and Wolf

The animal signs or totems also may be considered members of one of four clans—Tortoise, Butterfly, Hawk, or Frog. The signs of the element earth belong to the Tortoise clan, air to the Butterfly clan, fire to the Hawk clan, and water to the Frog clan. A *clan* is a family or group, which means that the signs belonging to the same clan have a particular affinity for each other, much as Aries (fire) has an affinity for Leo (fire).

The Four Winds

The four winds describe the four directions of the sky and divide the zodiac (the heavens) into four segments. Each direction rules three totems or astrological signs. The four winds symbolize knowledge and wisdom, both of which need to be integrated into one's character and life. The East Wind, the wind of spring (Falcon, Beaver, and Deer), supports astuteness and spirituality. The South Wind, the wind of summer (Woodpecker, Salmon, and Brown Bear), promotes perception and emotions. The West Wind, the wind of fall (Raven, Serpent, and Owl), promotes insight and knowledge. And the North Wind, the wind of winter (Goose, Otter, and Wolf), supports recuperation and renewal.

WHEEL OF THE FOUR WINDS

North Wind
Winter

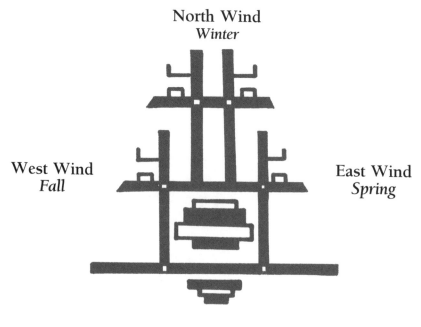

West Wind
Fall

East Wind
Spring

South Wind
Summer

14

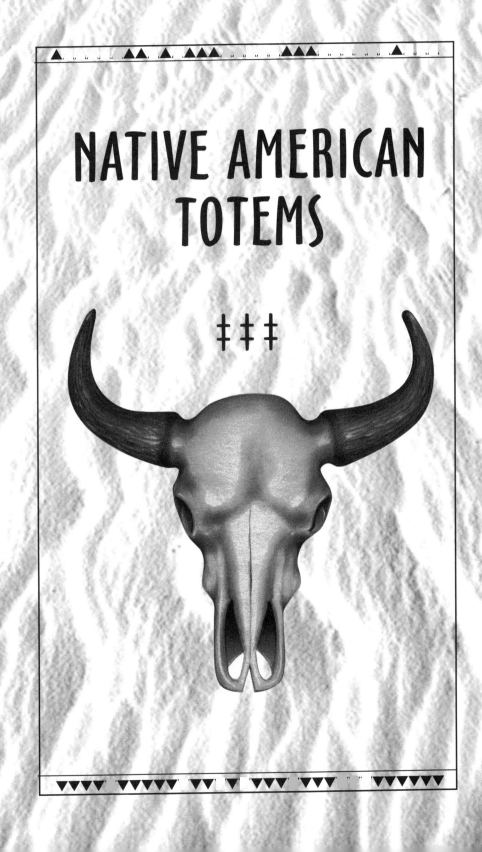

NATIVE AMERICAN TOTEMS

THE FALCON

MARCH 21–APRIL 19

Nature: *A Time of Awakening*

Animal Totem: *Falcon*

Element: *Fire*

Clan: *Hawk*

Wind: *East Wind*

Strengths: *Dynamism, Optimism*

Weaknesses: *Impulsiveness, Thoughtlessness*

The Animal Totem Falcon, a bird of prey, is as elegant as he is powerful. He is an excellent flier who catches his prey by nose-diving from great heights. His eyes express self-assurance, pride, and wisdom. Falcon has a curved beak and sharp talons which, when combined with his incredible speed and keen eyesight, make him an excellent hunter. Falcon symbolizes freedom and independence—the very reason it is so difficult to tame him.

The Element Falcon has been assigned the element fire, the element that stands for warmth, spirit, courage, and honesty. The influence of fire makes for an energetic and enthusiastic personality with strong emotions, spontaneity, and vitality. In other words, people born under the sign of Falcon are always ready to go and eager to game for adventure.

The Clan Falcon belongs to the Hawk clan. Members of this clan are the thinkers and the heroes. In other words, they are individuals who are self-assured and who want to inspire, convince, and move people. They want to lead. They are pioneers who blaze trails for others to follow. Motivated and inspired by a fire burning within, members of the Hawk clan are courageous and bold, and they never think small.

The Wind March 21 to April 19 is the time when the wind blows from the East, bringing spring and the promise of rebirth. The East is also where the Sun rises every day. The East Wind also symbolizes partings and new beginnings, typical for Falcon people. In nature new life awakens; for Falcon, new projects and ideas are created.

Falcon Character
People born under the sign of the Falcon are observant. However, given their temperament, they often lose sight of the big picture. They are always ready to rev up their engines. They focus quickly and spontaneously on a goal, sometimes overshooting their target. But who cares? Those who can catch themselves quickly can also just as quickly start over many times without much effort. In the end, everything works out. Confidence and drive, after all, are what count, and we can readily admire Falcon's vitality and enthusiasm.

Falcons love the excitement and tension of the moment; they do not make lengthy plans or devise complicated strategies. Rather, they are spontaneous and uncomplicated. Falcons know what they want and how to get it, even if their fiery temperament leads them into impulsive and exuberant action. But they are open, direct, and honest. Thanks to their down-to-earth charm, they are very endearing people. Count yourself lucky if you have Falcon as a friend. Those who make an enemy of him have only themselves to blame.

On the negative side, Falcons may fight merely for the sake of fighting. Also not be overlooked is their tendency at times to be egotistical and inconsiderate. Falcons need to learn to compromise and to accept the opinions of others.

Love
Falcon people, being influenced by the element fire, are very passionate. As they are in life, so they are in love–spontaneous and intense. They are most excited when falling in love, but it is not easy for them to maintain that level of excitement over the long haul, particularly when asked to make a long-term commitment. For that reason, Falcons often have to deal with the problem of infidelity.

These passionate people, capable of strong and intense emotions,

would do well to give expression to their emotions, because otherwise their emotions might be discharged in uncontrolled ways. That brings us to the subject of sexuality. Sexuality plays an important role in the life of Falcons. They can become passionately involved rather quickly, but they are, at the same time, also very romantic.

Although they are protective of their independence, they can be very jealous because they have a high opinion of themselves and want their partner to agree.

Career People born under the sign of the Falcon can go far in their chosen profession. They must have a certain amount of independence and the authority to make decisions. Since realistic planing or methodical preparation and the necessary staying power are sometimes lacking, Falcons may choose the wrong profession. They will, however, keep on searching and changing jobs as often as necessary until the right one comes along. Then they will totally dedicate themselves to this work, because, whatever they do, Falcons must be engaged body and soul. They do well in management positions because they have the gift of inspiring their employees to do their absolute best.

Vitality It is not unusual for Falcons to create performance and time pressures for themselves, because they often bite off more than they can chew—more than Falcon's constitution allows. This limits their endurance and energy. Sadly, these active personalities don't think much about taking a creative break. Thus they exhaust themselves unnecessarily.

Since the head is associated with this sign, Falcons often suffer from headaches or migraines. The element fire makes them easily irritated, which can raise blood pressure and cause sudden ailments or infections.

The Young Falcon

Typical Falcon characteristics can be detected at a tender age. If a Falcon child's demands are not met, he simply has a temper tantrum. Patience was certainly not invented by this little bundle of dynamite. What is much more likely is that, in the quest to satisfy his need to be active and on the move, he ends up with a few bumps and bruises. After all, the young Falcon has a lot of energy and loves to measure himself against others. It would be to everybody's advantage if early on this lively child is given the opportunity to let off steam with physical or athletic activities.

"I want" and "I want it now" are, by the way, the young Falcon's favorite phrases. That makes it difficult for parents to teach discipline and consideration. Not an easy undertaking! But the young Falcon is very receptive to a well-balanced combination of gentleness and firmness. Sooner or later he will be good-natured and obliging.

In spite of all that has been said so far about the young Falcon, he is a delightful child: open, honest, lovable, and almost always happy. In other words, a bundle of joy. Lots of outdoor activity as well as age-appropriate responsibilities that challenge his energy will help him to integrate his exuberance. By the way, he loves adventure stories, and parents should not deprive him of them. Such stories will engage his imagination and release some of his excess steam.

The Falcon and His or Her Partner

FALCON AND FALCON

Two Falcons not only share the same totem but also the element fire. A certain amount of agreement can be taken for granted. However, both are powerful people who have lots of drive and assertiveness and rather little patience. This is probably their greatest problem. On the other hand, both can move mountains.

FALCON AND BEAVER

While both signs have the East Wind in common—which gives them a positive attitude toward life—the somewhat more deliberate Beaver might interfere with Falcon's need to be active. On the other hand, Beaver might influence Falcon to be more constructive and productive. As a compensation, however, Falcon would have to slow down every now and then.

FALCON AND DEER

Here the East Wind and the elements fire and air promise that this couple will get along well and have a positive and fulfilling relationship. The vitality of Falcon and the rich ingenuity of Deer complement each other, and boredom seems foreign. This pair can be creative professionally and personally.

FALCON AND WOODPECKER

This combination could be problematic. The water element of Woodpecker extinguishes the fire element of Falcon. On the other hand, the fire might simply cause the water to evaporate. Good intentions alone will not suffice. In such a relationship, Falcon needs to be more considerate and Woodpecker more open. These requirements are precisely what both partners find so difficult to exercise.

FALCON AND SALMON

Salmon will have few problems adjusting to and becoming involved with Falcon, and vice versa. The element of fire, to which both belong, provides a good foundation. Also, their personalities and temperaments complement each other. It is only dominance or the need for both to be the leader that may cause some frustration. They combine East and South Winds, spring and summer.

FALCON AND BROWN BEAR

At first sight, these two won't be very receptive toward each other. The fiery temperament of Falcon will most likely turn off the earth-bound and steady Brown Bear. But it is worthwhile for both to give the relationship a chance. Falcon's bold plans could have a solid foundation when supported by Brown Bear.

FALCON AND RAVEN

The East Wind of Falcon, which brings initiative, could prove problematic for the West Wind of Raven, which indicates holding back and vice versa. At the same time, Falcon's element, fire, and Raven's element, air, do complement each other. But in spite of this, both partners must work to create a harmonious relationship. Falcon is the quintessential single warrior, and Raven the diplomatic team member. Such a combination requires compromise.

FALCON AND SERPENT

This is a combination of two deeply emotional and passionate people. Their partnership can be delightful as well as intriguing. Fire and water relationships always tend to be problematic. Due to their respective elements, they might not be able to find common ground. The emotional spontaneity of Falcon can present a great contradiction to the deep and complicated emotions of Serpent.

FALCON AND OWL

Owl, also ruled by the element fire, can truly enrich the life of Falcon. Falcon, full of idealism, could quickly ignite Owl's enthusiasm and passion. Together they will set out to conquer the world. Even on the less glamorous, private, and domestic side of life very few of their desires will remain unfulfilled.

FALCON AND GOOSE

A relationship between Falcon and Goose is certainly one in which common ground can be found. Both feel strong determination and the need for achievement. However, the way a given action or project is approached is quite different for each—which could spell trouble. The combination of fire and earth always requires concessions, and neither Falcon nor Goose does well in that department.

FALCON AND OTTER

While their ruling winds—East and North—blow in different directions, the elements fire and air provide Falcon and Otter a promising foundation. It should not be too difficult for Falcon to get excited about the plans and ideas of Otter. He can even be helpful in making them come true. Otter, in turn, will repay Falcon with sincere, heartfelt openness and with an abundance of ideas that promise fun, excitement, and entertainment for a long, long time.

FALCON AND WOLF

Wolf is smart but also very sensitive and, therefore, cautious, a characteristic Falcon might not necessarily understand. Here is another meeting between fire and water. But there is something that unites them: the hope Wolf brings and the knowledge Falcon supplies. And both realize that nature is about to create new life, a season of rebirth, spring.

THE BEAVER
APRIL 20–MAY 20

Nature: A Time of Growth

Animal Totem: Beaver

Element: Earth

Clan: Tortoise

Strengths: Steadfastness, Consistency

Weaknesses: Stubbornness, Limited Expression

The Animal Totem

The Beaver is a stocky, sturdy, and industrious animal who creates natural ponds in his environment. This rodent, a mammal, lives on land as well as in the water. Beaver is the engineer of the animal kingdom who, for his own security and comfort, changes his environment. Time and again Beavers expand and alter their habitat. Such industrious activities require great perseverance.

The Element

Beaver has been assigned the element earth, an element that indicates consistency, stability, steadfastness, and dependability. Earth is what supports life and provides security. It is, therefore, not surprising that people born under the sign of the Beaver are, more than anybody else, thought of as dependable. However, they often give too much importance to the material side of life, because of their need for security.

The Clan

Beaver belongs to the Tortoise clan. The Tortoise clan and element earth make sense for this sensitive animal because it wears a slick, protective fur. Protection and security are very important for members of the Tortoise clan. These people need a solid foundation in order to be active and to be able to grow. They want to build and preserve.

The Wind

During the period from April 20 to May 20, the wind blows from the east. While the East Wind indicates the time of awakening (Falcon) and the budding of trees—breaking through—this is the time when nature attends to strengthening the roots of plants and trees and providing protection for new animal life. Consequently, Beaver people prefer to be involved with practical, tangible, real things instead of theories or ideals.

Beaver Character
The time of the Beaver is the height of spring, when seeds sprout and seedlings take root. Strong, well-established roots make it possible for the newly sprouted buds and plants to grow in the soil. Beaver people need firm ground under their feet in all areas and situations in their life, and they are always trying to be sure of the outcome of what they do. They need a solid foundation from which they can grow and fulfill their dreams. They are sensible in all things.

Like the totem animal, Beavers are industrious and untiring while remaining levelheaded. They are dedicated to the job at hand, always trying to do justice to the task and reach their personal goal. In the end, Beaver people can be proud of what they have accomplished and acquired. They know what they want and go after it with patience and tenacity.

Their strong need for security and stability, influenced by the element earth, might make them inflexible. Beavers are often too focused on a specific subject, and this might diminish their ability to see the bigger picture. That, in turn, might mean that they miss great opportunities, not the least because Beavers hate to take risks since that could jeopardize the security they seek. Last but not least, Beavers relish comfort and are very sensual—a characteristic that finds its expression in their sexuality.

Love
The need Beavers have for security and stability also expresses itself in matters of love. For that reason, Beavers are as faithful as they are caring. Constantly changing partners is not their cup of tea since that would only create unrest in their life. Beaver people can be every now and then really stubborn people, and this is not always conducive to harmonious relationships.

Giving in is difficult. It will be good if the partner they choose has a knack for compromise and diplomacy. Of course, this should never go

so far as to let Beaver always have his own way.

People born under the sign of the Beaver are not necessarily passionate lovers, but they make up for it by being sensual. Romantic and tender physical contact provide a sense of security and safety. The lack of tender, generous caresses and cuddling will make Beavers feel more frustration than lust. After all, sexuality belongs to the creature comforts of life and must be savored with all the senses.

Career In their professional and work life, Beaver people are not necessarily interested in status. It is more important that the money is right. As industrious and determined as they are, they will make certain that that is the case. Beavers are reliable, stable, and hard-working; whatever the responsibility or task, it will be carried out with thoroughness. By the way, Beavers feel comfortable in professions that have to do with the Earth, like agriculture. They are good in handling money and also do well in banking, accounting, and related professions.

Vitality In general, people born under the sign of the Beaver are energetic, vigorous, and resilient. However, they love comfort, which includes good food and drink. Problems with weight are not uncommon if they indulge too much too often. In addition, problems in the area of the neck are not uncommon for Beavers. Tonsillitis and hoarseness are also more common for them than for people born under other signs.

The Young Beaver In general, the young Beaver is a well-behaved child who gives great joy to his parents because of his happy and positive disposition. Patient, like all Beavers, he does fine playing by himself for hours. But the need for material security is also very strong early on,

so that even at a tender age he will be possessive and strong-willed. When raising a young Beaver, it is important to make him understand that he won't lose anything by sharing and that he needs to learn to accept the opinions and needs of other people. As with the young Falcon, here, too, it is important that parents be gentle and consistent. Other than that, this happy, creative, and sociable child won't cause a lot of problems for his parents. Once in school, he works hard and shows healthy ambition. He is not necessarily a fast but rather a thorough learner, which means it is important for parents and teachers to give him enough time to understand and finish his assignments.

With increasing age and maturity, the young Beaver develops a considerable amount of independence and learns to put his talents to good use. Parents won't have to be quite as concerned, as is the case for children born under most of the other signs. It is very important, however, that he is allowed to develop within a consistent, predictable structure. This child needs clear boundaries and rules that he can understand, in order to follow them.

The Beaver and His or Her Partner

BEAVER AND FALCON

Beaver is influenced by the element earth and needs security, stability, and a loving home. Taken together, these are needs that Falcon, ruled by fire, is not necessarily able to comprehend, let alone fulfill. For that reason, both need to work hard to make the relationship work, and a big spark may not be enough.

BEAVER AND BEAVER

This combination is ideal in personal as well as business relationships. The element earth, influencing both, unites them in their need for security and stability. Beaver and Beaver can trust each other in almost all circumstances, and that's not a bad starting point for a long-lasting relationship. Only the lack of flexibility that afflicts both could at times lead to confrontations.

BEAVER AND DEER

The amiable Deer—whether Doe or Stag—is truly a jack-of-all-trades. Always active (especially mentally), endowed with many interests, always on the go, and looking for variety, she wants to get to know places and people. This could be a problem for the steady, earthbound Beaver, who needs a familiar rhythm in his life. But for Beaver to be more flexible won't do him any harm either.

BEAVER AND WOODPECKER

In each other, Beaver and Woodpecker find everything they desire in a partner, because the elements earth and water, present the best promise for optimal compatibility. They will be able to find common ground where it counts most. Beaver provides stability for Woodpecker, which he requires, and Woodpecker will thank her with affection and devotion.

BEAVER AND SALMON

This is a relationship of opposites, which cannot easily be bridged. That's because both Salmon and Beaver are not very good when it comes to tolerance and understanding. The elements fire and earth require compromise. On the other hand, both love the good things in life, which could provide a good foundation for their relationship.

BEAVER AND BROWN BEAR

Beaver and Brown Bear are ideal partners because they share the element earth. In addition, their personalities and both their rational and emotional needs are very similar. The only danger is that all this harmony could invite occasional boredom. But this is a small risk because Beaver and Brown Bear usually choose to be actively engaged in matters that interest both.

BEAVER AND RAVEN

Raven is not unsympathetic to Beaver since Raven, thanks to his quick and agreeable nature, has no difficulty accommodating the needs of Beaver. This, however, does not mean that an understanding on a deeper level is reached automatically, since earth and air need time to become familiar with each other and time to build trust.

BEAVER AND SERPENT

Without a doubt, tension is a given in this relationship, which could also make for a certain attraction between the two. But it could also prove to be very taxing. While earth and water complement each other, the personality traits as well as interests of Beaver and Serpent are very different. This often makes people vacillate between extremes and, indeed, between love and hate.

BEAVER AND OWL

Without question, Owls are very interesting and attractive. However, it is not always possible for the earthbound Beaver to be comfortable with the high ideals and expectations of Owl. The many contradictions likely to be part of this relationship have the potential to prevent it from becoming a fulfilling one. Good intentions alone may not be enough.

BEAVER AND GOOSE

Goose, like Beaver, is influenced by the element earth and for that reason alone a satisfying and harmonious relationship is almost guaranteed. They will understand each other immediately. No wonder: both have very similar personalities. Since both Goose and Beaver agree on the material things in life and are successful in pursuing and acquiring them, this combination is also interesting and lucrative in professional and business endeavors. They also agree on other substantive matters.

BEAVER AND OTTER

Beaver stands with both feet solidly on the ground while Otter, who is usually full of fun, lives in more lofty spheres. It goes without saying that in this relationship many difficulties need to be overcome. Both Beaver and Otter must work on the relationship. But there is a chance that over time the differences may even serve as an inspiration for both.

BEAVER AND WOLF

Beaver will warm up to Wolf in a hurry! And no wonder—Wolf, influenced by the element water, is sensitive and compassionate. She not only knows the desires of Beaver but also how to fulfill them. Wolf will waste few words; one look and she knows. However, Beaver should never become possessive, trying to keep Wolf all to himself.

THE DEER

MAY 21–JUNE 20

Nature: *A Time of Blooming*

Animal Totem: *Deer*

Element: *Air*

Clan: *Butterfly*

Wind: *East Wind*

Strengths: *Versatility, Agility*

Weakness: *Superficiality*

The Animal Totem

The family of the Deer has members that come in many different shapes, sizes, and weights. Deer, whether Doe or Stag, is a graceful, agile, and skillful animal who observes his environment with a quick, watchful eye and, if necessary, moves with lightning speed. He gives the impression of great intelligence. Stag is intelligent enough to avoid unnecessary confrontations or fights, except during rutting season.

The Element

Deer has been assigned the element air, which accounts for his characteristic nimbleness and quick movements. Deer's quickness is like the wind that stands between and connects everything. He is restless and untiring. This may account for the fact that a person born under the sign of the Deer wants to be everywhere at the same time and is always hoping to change things.

The Clan

Deer belongs to the Butterfly clan, which is ruled by the element air. The Butterfly is the symbol for being easy and carefree. The Butterfly moves constantly from flower to flower. Nowhere will Deer linger for very long. When applied to Stag people, this means that they impulsively satisfy their need for stimulation, diversion, and communication, since they feel so much in life needs to be discovered.

The Wind

The period between May 21 and June 20 is when the wind comes from the East, where the Sun rises. This always symbolizes a new beginning. But soon the wind will change direction and blow from the South. Spring is past its high point, and summer is sending its first messengers. Great new things are in the making and Deers love to be part of this.

Deer Character

While Deer are very sensitive, they are also relaxed and carefree. Deer need stimulating changes, which accounts for their urge to constantly force changes, great and small, on their environment to make life as interesting and colorful as possible. Long periods of quiet that might provide welcome rest make Deer nervous. They suffer when things are calm.

Deer people are open-minded and intellectually awake, which makes them fascinating company. They're clever and quick-witted. Flexibility and quick reactions are their strength, and they value open communication greatly. This is one of the main reasons they have no trouble making contact with other people. Since both Does and Stags are also slightly impatient, they do not hesitate during a heated debate to cut somebody off in mid-sentence.

Reacting quickly is second nature to people born under the animal totem and astrological sign of the Deer. The downside is that they are often seen as capricious and fickle because they do not always take time to explore a subject in depth.

They know how to get the attention of the people around them with charm and flair, thereby making up for a volatile and capricious nature. But it still would be sad if the changes and stimulations they seek never go beyond the superficial.

Love

Deer people are commonly considered happy-go-lucky. Since they have a penchant for diversion, it could be difficult for them to settle down to a long-term relationship, unless the partner knows how to always keep their love life interesting, exciting, and stimulating. This is surely not an easy assignment.

But even if a partner does all that, Stag or Doe will, every now and then, let his or her eyes roam and not shy away from a little flirting. For that reason, the partner not only needs to be interesting, but also tolerant. While Deer people—contrary to other tendencies—won't make serious commitments easily, they are masters of flirtation, courtship, and seduction. Stag and Doe easily charm the opposite sex to submission with elegance. An unforgettable night of love-making is often preceded by an enjoyable, stylish evening entertainment and, of course, stimulating conversation. This much is certain: love and marriage with a Deer person will never be boring as long as it is based on tolerance. That is the key to happiness with Stag or Doe.

Career Because their curious minds need the challenge of intellectually stimulating work, Deer attach great importance to a job that is complex and exciting. In addition, Deer, who are considerably talented in business, can be diplomatic negotiators. Professions that require contact with the public and include frequent business trips, like positions in sales or journalism, are especially suitable. It's important that Deer work where things are happening. That's because they react to boredom quite badly, at work and in private life.

Vitality From a physical point of few, the most vulnerable areas of Deer are the respiratory system, the nervous system, the arms, and the hands. It is important for Deer with a cold to make sure that he is fully recovered before resuming normal activities, so that the lungs and bronchial tubes won't become infected. Since Stags and Does are often in overdrive and have a tendency to create more stress than they can tolerate, it is particularly important that they make every effort to take breaks and to relax.

The Young Deer

A young Deer is a very active, bright, and vibrant child who is open to everything around him and, therefore, highly stimulated by his environment. Parents do well to provide what is necessary, if the child is not capable of creating it himself. This is particularly the case in school and when studying. While the young Fawn is bright, loves to learn, and can take in a considerable amount of material, his concentration and patience do not always keep pace. Learning comes easily and quickly, but it can also be somewhat superficial. This child needs to be encouraged to look under the surface of things.

One of the positive traits of the young Fawn is that he knows how to spread cheer and make people happy. From his very early days he is a fabulous entertainer who loves to talk. This need and his enjoyment of people should be supported by his parents. But it is equally important that he be taught to take people seriously and to allow them to finish their sentences.

Imagination and expressiveness are well developed in this child. He loves exciting stories and will, if necessary, invent them. Make sure that his nursery school and his room always have appropriate books on the shelf. He loves it when his mom or dad reads to him from these books at bedtime, preferably allowing time to talk about what he has heard. Then he can finally get to sleep. Settling down and getting to sleep is difficult for him, so his parents need to be prepared. Make sure that bedtime stories are not too exciting and stimulating, but they also must not be too boring.

The Deer and His or Her Partner

Deer and Falcon The elements air and fire could create intense heat, and Deer would surely love to be conquered and seduced by Falcon. In addition, such a relationship is rich in ideas and dynamic activities. Whatever the Deer can conceive, the Falcon will carry out. Here not only will love prosper, but joint projects and plans will also.

Deer and Beaver In the beginning these two signs won't suffer from sleepless nights. Deer is loose and carefree, and Beaver stands on solid ground. Since they are both so different, they may complement and enrich each other. But there is no guarantee they'll live happily ever after. Whatever else is required, both must be willing to compromise.

Deer and Deer When people of the same element and the same sign meet, a great deal of accord can be expected. And, indeed, two Deer can have much fun together and constantly stimulate each other. Their relationship will be interesting and exciting. But too much intellectual excitement and diversion could mean lack of emotional depth.

Deer and Woodpecker The elements air (Deer) and water (Woodpecker) are strangers. While Woodpecker builds a comfortable nest, hoping that her love will feel at home, Stag roams about and might forget to come home. Under such circumstances, one cannot hope for a great deal of cooperation. However, in such a relationship Stag has a chance to learn something about deep emotions.

Deer and Salmon

Deer and Salmon, due to the harmonizing elements air and fire, tend to get along well, sometimes extremely well. They both love a certain amount of freedom and are always open to positive inspirations and diversions. The fact that Salmon loves to be the leader makes no difference to Deer. If it gets to be too much, she will simply take off for a few days.

Deer and Brown Bear

While Brown Bear could be an ideal companion, in the beginning Deer won't be overjoyed because the elements air and earth do not make an ideal mixture. Brown Bear, because he is so dutiful and principled, may spoil the fun for Doe and accuse her of being superficial. But there is one thing that does shine: they both have goodwill.

Deer and Raven

Here, again, are two signs that have the element air in common, which promises to be an interesting and stimulating combination. Both Deer and Raven have spirit and are very sociable. Not many desires will remain unfulfilled, if any at all. Only their strong leaning toward diversion could sooner or later create stress.

Deer and Serpent

The problem with this combination can be that Deer prefers to explore the obvious things in life while Serpent is more tuned to deep and secret areas. The question is whether the two elements, air and water, will meet on the intellectual or emotional plane. Under ideal circumstances, it won't be either-or but rather, both. That's not always easy.

Deer and Owl Apart from a few contradictory traits, people belonging to these signs should get along well. Deer believes in logic and knowledge, and Owl wants to discover and understand the wisdom behind the knowledge. If Deer is willing to engage in such deep intellectual endeavors, nothing will stand in the way of happiness.

Deer and Goose In the beginning, Deer has no idea of what to do with Goose, who belongs to the element earth. Deer is relaxed, agile, and sometimes even superficial. The strict and more focused Goose could serve as either a solid foundation for Deer or be a hindrance. This is the big question that both would do well to take the time to answer.

Deer and Otter Otter, another creature ruled by the element air, is just what Deer hopes to find. Pooling their strengths, these two could reach intellectual heights that could assume ever new dimensions. However, there is also the danger of canceling each other out. For that reason, Deer and Otter should make sure not to ignore the commonplace realities of life.

Deer and Wolf With Deer and Wolf, the elements air and water meet. The danger in this relationship is that both live separate lives because their needs are so different. They might not be able to understand each other, let alone find common ground, unless Stag, contrary to his usual habit, is willing to delve more deeply into his emotions and Wolf is willing to be more carefree.

THE WOODPECKER

JUNE 21–JULY 21

Nature: A Time of Consolidation

Animal Totem: Woodpecker

Element: Water

Clan: Frog

Wind: South Wind

Strengths: Sensitivity, Devotion

Weakness: Brooding

The Animal Totem

Woodpecker is a colorful bird with a sharp beak and curved, sharp claws. He digs his claws into the bark of a tree and uses his beak rhythmically, creating a sound difficult to ignore. The sound, reminiscent of a drumbeat, reveals that he is either looking for food or building a nest. His nest is very comfortable and protected. Safety and security are urgent needs for people born under the sign of the Woodpecker.

The Element

Woodpecker is influenced by the element water, which is connected to the emotions. Woodpecker's intense emotions need to be expressed in profusion. Water can also stir sensibilities that may grow into extreme sensitivity. This may be why Woodpecker people often are wary.

The Clan

Woodpecker belongs to the Frog clan. Members of this clan should always allow themselves to express their feelings and try to be aware of their unconscious needs. If they fail to do so, unexpressed emotions may build up and explode suddenly and uncontrollably. Frog people are particularly empathetic and very creative. Woodpeckers are open to great inspirations.

The Wind

During the period between June 21 and July 21, the wind blows from the South and brings summer to places north of the Equator. The immense energy and comfortable warmth of the Sun has been inherited by Woodpeckers, even though they are unaware of it. Because they are influenced by the element water and need to be emotionally protected, they tend to be cautious and introverted. They need time to

discover and accept the natural light within themselves. With self-confidence they can grow into their true selves.

Woodpecker Character

Woodpecker is a sensitive and empathetic person who depends on his emotions. Without emotional involvement, nothing seems to be happening in his life. His emotional sensitivity makes for a very poignant core in need of protection. Woodpeckers carefully protect their boundaries until they feel they can trust people and situations. Only then are they willing to be emotionally present. Woodpeckers do not only look at their experiences with their intellect, they often reach deep into the psyche where they create happiness as well as chaos. This accounts for their great mood fluctuations.

To protect themselves, Woodpeckers often pretend to be aloof. Sometimes people think they are unapproachable—even though their emotions churn inside and readily connect with others. Woodpeckers' emotions are felt deeply. That's why they long for security and always look for people they can trust. The element water also influences their need for affection. People born under the sign of the Woodpecker need to be needed. They can develop a remarkable ability of caring for their fellow men, particularly for family members and friends.

This need to help others, however, is often overdone. It makes Woodpeckers cling too tightly to the comfortable environment—in the bird's case, a tree—they are familiar with. While Woodpeckers ought to enjoy their domesticity, they also must learn not to be too helpful to those closest to them. They can be taken advantage of.

Love

Deep and intense are Woodpecker's feelings. They take love very seriously. Playing with fire, flirting, and amorous adventures are not their cup of tea. Having chosen a partner, they will pledge themselves to that

person body and soul. They will be faithful, devoted, and try everything to fulfill the desires and needs of their partner—usually with great success.

Woodpeckers need safety and security in their relationship. They need lots of hugs, strokes, and cuddling; tenderness and romance are what they look for in a love relationship. Overly passionate and wild loving is almost a turnoff. Harmony and fulfillment will depend to a great degree on how much time is set aside for undisturbed hours together. They expect exactly what they are more than willing to give themselves: undivided attention and gentle caring. Their biggest problem might be that they are too sensitive. Woodpeckers are easily offended and often react with being overly sensitive and moody.

Career People born under the sign of the Woodpecker do not necessarily look for a career. Power, influence, and social prestige are kept in normal limits. What Woodpeckers need most of all is a job that is fulfilling and satisfying. They need a working environment where they can be comfortable. A small, respected company with a friendly boss and a few nice co-workers is just the right setting. The climate in the office is particularly important; a somewhat familiar, comfortable, and even homelike setting is what they like best. That notwithstanding, Woodpeckers are very capable and work hard. Once given a responsibility, they are engaged heart and mind. Bosses or supervisors regret losing them.

Vitality In spite of the fact that Woodpeckers are sometimes moody, they have a remarkably resilient constitution, even though they react to pain more strongly than other people. From a physical point of view, the stomach, chest, and breasts are the most vulnerable. The stomach gives them the most trouble because they have a tendency to swallow frustration and anger.

The Young Woodpecker

The young Woodpecker is by nature a very peaceful child who won't ask constantly for attention. Thanks to his considerable imagination, he loves to entertain himself with things in his environment; parents would do well to support his creativity. Since he is very sensitive, the young Woodpecker needs to know that somebody is always close by, preferably his mother. Harsh words are difficult for him to deal with. They make him sad and tend to cause him to withdraw. It is very important that parents raise this child with understanding. This is not to imply that parents should not be consistent. Strictness is seldom necessary, because Woodpecker children are rarely stubborn. They would never jeopardize the love of their parents.

From a very early age, fledgling Woodpeckers need security and a sense of safety. This child should be cared for and nurtured with a firm but loving hand. Most of all, they need to be encouraged to trust themselves, because young Woodpeckers are rarely very self-confident or assertive.

The young Woodpecker enjoys both school and learning, but much depends on his teachers. Sensitive as this little Woodpecker is, much of his success depends on how well he likes his teacher. This quiet dependency that will diminish, more or less, as he gets older.

The Woodpecker and His or Her Partner

WOODPECKER AND FALCON

Woodpecker will be overwhelmed by the dynamism and spontaneity of Falcon. Woodpecker will be pleasantly surprised by Falcon's many talents, which he does not have. A harmonious relationship, however, is still not guaranteed. For a relationship to succeed, many differences must be overcome.

WOODPECKER AND BEAVER

Beaver, a representative of the element earth, complements Woodpecker's interests, desires, and needs. Both signs are domestic and caring; that's why they understand and indulge each other. The quiet strength of the reliable Beaver is food for Woodpecker's soul. Tenderness and romance will flower in this relationship.

WOODPECKER AND DEER

The sensitive Woodpecker longs for human touch, warmth, security, and a comfortable home. Stag's needs are quite different. He requires much personal freedom in order to satisfy his need for distraction, contact, and communication with other people. Woodpecker will quickly feel sad, neglected, and suffer quietly with the energetic, roving Deer.

WOODPECKER AND WOODPECKER

This double-dose of the element water helps create a strong and intense relationship. Woodpecker and Woodpecker, due to their innate sensitivity, understand each other without words. Their emotional traits are very much alike; one could envy their harmony. While their relationship may lack dynamism, they don't care.

WOODPECKER AND SALMON

Salmon, influenced by the element fire, is considered forceful, even domineering. On one hand, this could bother Woodpecker. On the other hand, Salmon radiates warmth and affection, traits Woodpecker delights in with all his heart. People born under the sign of the Woodpecker will, for just that reason, usually accept Salmon's leadership.

WOODPECKER AND BROWN BEAR

The two elements water and earth provide a harmonious and stable foundation for a fulfilling relationship. Brown Bear has a good grasp on reality and always remains practical. He can, therefore, provide good support for the sometimes moody Woodpecker. Also, the sensitive and emotionally engaged Woodpecker can coax the reserved Brown Bear out of his cave.

WOODPECKER AND RAVEN

While air (Raven) is able to move or even stir up water (Woodpecker), it cannot penetrate water's depth. That's why Ravens and Woodpeckers have such difficulty finding common ground. They need something they both value to help balance the needs of both the soul and the intellect. If they are successful, they can learn much from each other and outgrow individual limitations.

WOODPECKER AND SERPENT

These two totems or signs not only have the element water in common, they'll also find perfect harmony in the characteristics they share. Both Woodpecker and Serpent are emotionally charged people, capable of very deep emotions. Such a couple can reach emotional and erotic states that others can only dream about.

WOODPECKER AND OWL

The warmth and security Woodpecker needs can easily be supplied by Owl. Ruled by the element fire, Owl brings to the relationship a warm glow. Owl is also spontaneous and needs personal freedom. In his search for the great big world and the meaning of life, Owl doesn't want to be tied down to a domestic life. That could create problems.

WOODPECKER AND GOOSE

While the elements water and earth get along well, contradictions between Woodpecker and Goose are a given, due to their strong and different personal interests and needs. In some instances, both complement each other, but the trick is to find a golden middle a workable solution. This includes the need to compromise.

WOODPECKER AND OTTER

A world could separate Woodpecker and Otter. While Woodpecker is a domestic and sensitive creature, highly influenced by emotions, Otter is more drawn to the intellectual and idealistic side of life. The question is: where can they meet? To avoid frustration, both partners need to exercise tolerance and forbearance.

WOODPECKER AND WOLF

Both Woodpecker and Wolf belong to the element water, making them both highly sensitive. This combination is truly a relationship where heart and soul act in harmony. Thanks to their silent understanding, no desire will remain unfulfilled.

THE SALMON

JULY 22—AUGUST 21

Nature: *A Time of Ripening*

Animal Totem: *Salmon*

Element: *Fire*

Clan: *Hawk*

Wind: *South Wind*

Strengths: *Self-Assurance, Warmth*

Weaknesses: *Egotism, Arrogance*

The Animal Totem
Salmon has been called the king of fish. No wonder! This animal grows to over 48 inches (120 centimeters) long and can weigh as much as 65 pounds (30 kilograms). In addition, Salmon moves through the water with an elegance and grace that we cannot help but admire. On his long journey upstream and far from his ocean home to spawning grounds, he overcomes all obstacles silently, easily, and with dignity.

The Element
Salmon is influenced by the element fire, which gives Salmon people their inner strength, passion, and innate power. Salmons have fire in the heart. The element fire makes people born under the sign of the Salmon deeply affectionate and generous.

The Clan
Salmon belongs to the Hawk clan, a clan influenced by the element fire. Members of this clan are frank, open, and energetic people who have a healthy portion of ambition, thirst for action, and assertiveness. But the fire element can also make them too audacious. Members of this clan tend to overdo and often burn out. The trick is to reduce the roaring fire within to a more slow-burning flame in which energy can be used more sensibly and with less waste.

The Wind
The period between July 22 and August 21 is the time when the South Wind dominates. Salmon carry with them powerful energies and vitality, allowing people born under this sign to carry out commanding and responsible tasks. However, Salmon people do not suffer because of it, as might be the case with people born under other signs. On the contrary, they love to be out in front, and love a good fight.

The warmth they receive from being in the limelight coincides perfectly with their temperament.

Salmon Character

People born under the sign of the Salmon have what is commonly referred to as a strong personality. They are convinced of their own worth and act accordingly: self-confident, wise about the ways of the world and, sometimes, a bit arrogant. Salmon has a big heart and a sunny disposition that lets others know they can lean on him. Indeed, Salmon people make good protectors and are willing and able to lead. Their dynamic and positive attitude toward life and the influence of the element fire give them the necessary strength to take on the heavy but rewarding responsibilities required for many professional and social positions.

Emotionally as well as materially, Salmon people tend to draw from sources they believe to be unlimited. They express their emotions openly and with the same generosity they display in financial matters. However, they expect recognition or, better yet, admiration for what they do. It is the least they expect when they have made a decision or picked chestnuts out of the fire for somebody else. In turn, however, Salmon should not be surprised when they are seen as presumptuous. Such is usually the case when their innate leadership and spontaneous judgments lead them to overshoot the goal. Salmon people seem to think that they always know what is good for others, and often they are right. But they should never let it get so far as to make decisions for other people or force their own opinions and values on others.

Love

Bold, courageous, and passionate: that is how Salmon people not only approach life, but also love. Love for them is a way to give expression to their intense feelings. They go to great lengths to find favor with their partner and are never stingy with compliments, lovely promises, or generous gifts.

The love Salmon people experience is complete, and sex is very important to them. They did not invent platonic love. They want to experience their partner fully—intellectually, emotionally, and physically. In the heat of an amorous conquest, due to his passion and devotion, Salmon may try to possess a partner, which could get in the way of a harmonious relationship. Jealousy is a real problem. For Salmon people to have a fulfilling and happy relationship, they need to develop more patience and understanding or chose a partner who is submissive. But that also is not something Salmon dream about.

Career

It seems obvious that Salmon will not seek or accept a low rank in professional or working life. Healthy ambition, self-confidence, and competence will help assure that they can steadily move up the ladder to better positions. They feel most at home in places where strings can be pulled and important decisions made. They do not shy away from assuming responsibilities connected with those positions. Since people born under the sign of Salmon are always willing to take risks, they make excellent entrepreneurs who can create something from nothing and see important projects through to a successful conclusion. As bosses, they are tough but kind.

Vitality

People born under the sign of the Salmon usually have a healthy, robust constitution. Their vitality is just as remarkable as their zest for life. The latter is most likely the result of the former. If any health problem arise, they probably do because Salmon people miscalculate their energy reserves and go beyond what their bodies can deal with.

Physically, the problems most likely to develop in later life will be with the circulatory system and blood pressure. Salmon people are also prone to problems with the back, which requires special care.

The Young Salmon

Young Salmon, no matter how small, love to be the center of attention and treated royally by parents and all relatives. After all, there is nothing like getting a head start when the king fish's future goal is to be in the limelight. Of course, complete attention received is generously repaid with radiant smiles and joyful laughter that warms everyone's heart.

But parents beware! Don't be too overwhelmed by this sweet child! Rather, make sure that he learns to be considerate, disciplined, and tolerant. Otherwise, this child could develop into a little tyrant who has the whole family at his mercy. Fairness is another subject that the little Salmon must tackle. Furthermore, he should learn to rein in his big ego so that others also have a chance to be heard and receive what is rightfully due them.

Happily, the little Salmon is by nature kind and generous toward the world around him. He likes to give gifts and often makes sure, without being prompted, that others are not short-changed, even if he keeps the biggest cookie for himself.

In general, Salmon have no difficulties with their teachers; it is more the other way around, because they are self-assured from an early age. They do not hesitate to fight for their own and fellow students' rights. One can safely assume that leadership qualities begin to flower early in their life, which quickly make many young Salmon spokespeople for their school or fellow students.

The Salmon and His or Her Partner

SALMON AND FALCON

This is a relationship of two very temperamental and passionate people, who often like or even love each other at first sight. Falcon is sure to do justice to Salmon's expectations and to stand by him. Since both are determined and dominant people, it would serve them well to decide the rules of the game early. That way they will avoid unnecessary differences.

SALMON AND BEAVER

People influenced by the elements fire and earth may find themselves in a quandary. Both should be willing to compromise and lower the high expectations they have of the other. Unfortunately, both can be stubborn at times, which makes giving in difficult. But when it comes to being comfortable, both agree.

SALMON AND DEER

Salmon and Deer make a happy twosome who have no difficulty accommodating each other. The elements fire and air complement each other, as do their personalities. This almost guarantees that they will suffer no lack of stimulation. Deer, whether Stag or Doe, is very flexible and willing to compromise, giving the more dominant Salmon few problems.

SALMON AND WOODPECKER

The contradictions in this relationship cannot be denied even if, in the end, they provide an opportunity for mutual growth. Salmon is a natural leader who radiates kindness and warmth. He is a person one can lean on (if you are accommodating). And that is exactly what Woodpecker sometimes searches for. However, Salmon must try to be less dominant.

SALMON AND SALMON

Two Salmon together—what a strong team they can be! However, only if they are willing to develop a team spirit and avoid competing for leadership—after all, Salmon, ruled by fire, is a dominant personality. What's certain is that when these two meet, sparks will fly.

SALMON AND BROWN BEAR

Salmon loves to have people look up to him. Brown Bear is willing and able to do just that. However, it remains to be seen if that's sufficient for a happy and fulfilling relationship. It would be good if there were other aspects they can agree on. Searching for them wouldn't be an easy matter. Both Salmon and Brown Bear closely examine their situation before deciding to tie the knot.

SALMON AND RAVEN

The element air, which Raven supplies, literally brings a breath of fresh air into the life of Salmon. Fortunately, Raven has no intention of challenging the Salmon's leadership. This is a relationship in which harmony reigns. Salmon and Raven can create a satisfying, sophisticated lifestyle.

SALMON AND SERPENT

Since Serpent loves to delve into the subconscious and unfathomable secret subjects, Salmon might feel uncomfortable at times. Serpent has the uncanny ability to uncover peculiarities, sensitive subjects, and weaknesses—in other words: easily look behind Salmon's or anyone else's façade. It will not be easy to overcome a little mistrust in order to form a trusting relationship.

SALMON AND OWL

Salmon will quickly fall in love with Owl. After all, they have the element fire in common. However, this fact alone does not guarantee a happy

relationship. Owl asks for a lot of freedom and independence—which requires trust and tolerance—and Salmon might at times have a problem granting her that.

SALMON AND GOOSE

Goose may appear alien to Salmon and little will change unless Salmon makes the effort to discover and understand the needs of Goose. While any effort Salmon makes would be richly rewarded, his automatic expectations and demands may get in the way.

SALMON AND OTTER

Since Otter loves freedom, independence, and self-sufficiency, he won't adapt to the rules of Salmon without taking a close look at the reasons behind them. This could easily lead to tension. Attraction or rejection depends to a large degree on how receptive and tolerant Salmon and Otter are with each other. While the dissimilarities cannot be denied, such a relationship also has great possibilities.

SALMON AND WOLF

While Wolf is often rough on the outside, he is also very soft inside, and that softness or gentleness could attract Salmon. No matter how much the Wolf leans on Salmon, he won't reveal everything. Wolf also holds many cards in his hand close to his chest. The question is: does Salmon have enough patience and empathy to understand Wolf?

THE BROWN BEAR

AUGUST 22–SEPTEMBER 21

Nature: A Time of Harvest

Animal Totem: Brown Bear

Element: Earth

Clan: Turtle

Wind: South Wind

Strength: Conscientiousness

Weakness: Pedantry, Criticism

The Animal Totem The considerable size and enormous power of Brown Bear should not overshadow the fact that he is a shy and very gentle creature, unless or until his life is threatened. Brown Bear, like humans, is also able to stand on two feet, and most of the time he seems to be good-natured and satisfied. One is almost tempted to take him for a reasonable, practical creature, because sometimes he appears to be almost human. Putting that aside, the Brown Bear is very adaptable; after all, people can train him.

The Element Brown Bear is influenced by the element earth. This element symbolizes steadfastness and reliability, and those born under this sign are stable people who are connected to nature. They feel most comfortable when they are at home in an ordered environment that is predictable and can be controlled.

The Clan Brown Bear belongs to the Turtle clan, which is also under the influence of the element earth. It accounts for the fact that people born under this sign need consistency and to be rooted, so that their lives can have a stable foundation. That is also why they are able to provide security, support, and stability for others. In addition, it is very important for Brown Bear people to maintain a strong connection to nature.

The Wind During the period between August 22 and September 21, the wind blows from the South, a direction that is closely connected with the energy of fire and the Sun. But temperatures during this period are not quite as intense anymore, and the air becomes more cool. While Brown Bears, on one hand, still draw from the abundance in nature, they are, on the other hand, also beginning to look ahead and deal analytically with future possibilities and developments.

Brown Bear Character
People born under the sign of the Brown Bear love to draw on their practical talents, using them rationally and in a very focused way to become as independent as possible. They do not like to rely on others. Generally, this means that they are very reliable and work hard. Since they are industrious and pursue their goals systematically and with perseverance, Brown Bears usually have a good eye for detail.

Brown Bears are restrained and modest. They do not seek the limelight. They take care of their responsibilities thoroughly and conscientiously, because that is how it is supposed to be. They also have a tendency to hide their light under the bushel basket. Since Brown Bears need a solid and controlled environment in which to live, they love to plan ahead. They often feel insecure when things are left to chance or something unexpected arises.

Brown Bears have a tendency toward perfectionism. Stress is no stranger because they ask much of themselves, often more than they can handle. Instead of doing everything 100 percent, they should try to learn to be less meticulous. Given those traits, Brown Bears do not hesitate to be critical. At times they can be rather pedantic, finding many things objectionable—a trait that makes them difficult to live with. A bit more tolerance would serve them well.

Love
Brown Bears do not like dramatic or spectacular entrances. They prefer to be observers and hold to a wait-and-see attitude. Even in matters of love, they don't show their emotions quickly. It is difficult for them to express deep and intense feelings. This kind of emotional reserve is

often misunderstood. But a partner who will take time to get to know a Brown Bear will not be disappointed. On the contrary: under this careful exterior are strong, tender, and romantic feelings—even a smidgen of passion.

Most important, however, is the fact that Brown Bears are dependable people. Marriage vows are taken very seriously, as is the belief that shared sorrow is half the sorrow. In other words, this is a partner who can share both good and difficult times in life.

Career

Brown Bears are dependable and hard-working and their ability to adapt is equally appreciated by bosses and colleagues. They acquire the necessary basic knowledge, do their work with precision, and produce good results. In spite of this, they are not driven to reach top management or other high positions. They much prefer to work behind the scenes in peace and quiet, since this accommodates their reserved nature. Besides, Brown Bears have the tendency to be helpful and to serve, which is why they are often found in service and healing professions.

Vitality

The greatest problem for Bear Bears is that they deny themselves many lovely things in life, which sometimes makes them dissatisfied. They do not deal well with stress, particularly when they have taken on more than their constitution allows. All of these reasons should be reason enough to give them permission to take life less seriously.

Physically, the stomach and digestive system are most vulnerable, areas that are particularly affected when they are emotionally dissatisfied. It behooves Brown Bear to pay attention to proper nutrition. Other than that, Brown Bears have a tendency to worry unnecessarily about their health.

The Young Brown Bear
Young Brown Bears are also undemanding, well-behaved children who are easy to take care of. These children almost seem sent from heaven, and their behavior is especially pleasing for parents with nervous dispositions. As children, Brown Bears do not like to make a big fuss, and they adapt relatively easily. For healthy development, little Brown Bears need most of all well-defined boundaries, consistency, well-ordered routines, and predictable surroundings.

The little Brown Bear cub's innate sense of responsibility allows parents to give him small and child-appropriate tasks, which he will carry out well and with great joy. But parents must also take care to assure that the playful side of his life is not neglected. Otherwise, he will not be a playful child but become too serious, like a small adult.

Young Brown Bears, like adult Brown Bears, also tend to minimize their many good qualities and talents. They are very modest. For that reason, it is important that parents give them a sense of self-worth with lots of encouragement and praise. Parents should also make sure that Little Brown Bears learn to trust their own feelings; otherwise, they may fail to think with both heart and head.

Little Brown Bears are eager and willing to learn, which makes school years very positive. For young Bears, learning is not burdensome; it's fun. What a lucky person! After all, knowledge is power and a prerequisite for a productive life. The Brown Bear cub also has no problem with authority, because decisions, which he dislikes anyway, are made for him.

The Brown Bear and His or Her Partner

BROWN BEAR AND FALCON

Brown Bear, connected to nature and Mother Earth as he is, loves an orderly life that moves in quiet and predictable ways. But when Falcon, ruled by fire, crosses his path, peace and quiet cease. The dynamic, power-packed Falcon brings more energy to the life of Brown Bear than he can stand. Both have to work hard to keep the relationship harmonious.

BROWN BEAR AND BEAVER

Both signs and animal totems are ruled by the element earth, which should make a good relationship, at least as it touches on basic issues and needs. Industrious and hard-working, Brown Bear finds a dependable and faithful partner in Beaver, who will share with him the comforts and beauty in life.

BROWN BEAR AND DEER

Deer, due to his innate inclinations and intellectual excitement, may well create a restlessness that Brown Bear, with his need for a steady, practical, and well-ordered life, may find unsettling. Brown Bear and Deer will have a hard time reconciling their differences. Good communication may be the only way to overcome these obstacles.

BROWN BEAR AND WOODPECKER

Brown Bear and Woodpecker have a good foundation, based on their respective elements, earth and water. They complement and understand each other without many words: Brown Bear takes care of a stable environment and Woodpecker, sensitive and emotionally devoted, provides trust. Both will be fulfilled because they enrich each other's lives.

BROWN BEAR AND SALMON

Due to the influence of the element fire, Salmon brings deep emotions and a happy disposition to this relationship, which Brown Bear really likes. However, the Salmon also has rather high expectations both of life and love, something the more reserved Brown Bear may not appreciate enough. These two people may have widely differing opinions and ideas. Compromising may bridge the gap.

BROWN BEAR AND BROWN BEAR

The element earth, which both Brown Bears share, provides a solid base for their relationship, and their tendencies and interests are also much alike. What may be missing in this relationship is emotional spontaneity, because both express their emotions in more measured ways.

BROWN BEAR AND RAVEN

Brown Bear prefers to stand with both feet on the solid ground of facts. While he is not a loner, he does love home life and a certain amount of seclusion. For Raven, this is often hard to understand because he loves diversion and is very social. If Brown Bear can show more flexibility and Raven more willingness to curtail some of his inclinations, this may not be a bad combination.

BROWN BEAR AND SERPENT

In this relationship, Brown Bear may enjoy the fact that Serpent is somebody who rattles his chains. On one hand, Serpent, due to the influence of the element water, is an emotionally charged person who knows how to coax Brown Bear out of his emotional reserve. On the other hand, the sometimes highly independent Brown Bear may be a welcome challenge to Serpent.

BROWN BEAR AND OWL

While Brown Bear does not always agree with the circumstances and realities of life, he can at least respect them—something that is very difficult for Owl because he always looks for superlatives. Mutually agreeable compromises and harmony in this partnership will be difficult to achieve.

BROWN BEAR AND GOOSE

The situation of Brown Bear and Owl is not what troubles this relationship. Goose, like Brown Bear, is influenced by the element earth and, therefore, remains a solid, steadfast, peaceful, and strong person. Goose and Brown Bear operate on the same wavelength. However, they often view life more seriously than necessary. Both should make sure that fun and trust in the positive things in life are not short-changed.

BROWN BEAR AND OTTER

Brown Bear and Otter might as well live on different planets. The elements that influence their respective signs, earth and air, make understanding each other difficult. The Brown Bear wants to preserve and stabilize the world, Otter wants to change and reform it. They begin from widely differing concepts. However, when both are willing to communicate, the results can be very good.

BROWN BEAR AND WOLF

While the elements earth and water may serve as a basis for mutual growth, tension in this relationship is a given. That's because Brown Bear is primarily ruled by his head, while Wolf is guided by emotions and trusts her instincts—something of which Brown Bear is suspicious.

THE RAVEN

SEPTEMBER 22–October 22

Nature: *A Time of Retreat*

Animal Totem: *Raven*

Element: *Air*

Clan: *Butterfly*

Wind: *West Wind*

Strengths: *Cooperation, Diplomacy*

Weaknesses: *Indecision, Naïveté*

The Animal Totem

The Raven, with his black feathers—singed from bringing stolen fire back into the world—and his large beak and powerful legs, easily adapts to any situation. His strength allows him to handle almost anything. Generally, Ravens search for food in pairs or groups and even share sleeping quarters, at least during winter months. While many Westerners have considered Raven a plague, Native Americans recognize that this carrion-eater represents a balancing agent in nature. Raven is an intelligent and capable bird, one who moves adroitly both in the air and on the ground.

The Element

Raven is influenced by the element air. The air we breathe, which maintains human life and those of all plants and animals around us, has many different qualities. Air ranges from mild and refreshing to wild and stormy. Since air connects us to the world and encourages association, people born under the sign of Raven are anything but solitary. They are quite sociable and friendly, circulating like the air.

The Clan

Raven belongs to the Butterfly clan, which has an affinity with the element air. This makes members of this clan active, not just physically but intellectually. Their intellectual exercises produce interesting ideas and conversations. This is why they have a very stimulating effect on their surroundings. Butterflies keep everything in motion—which also means that they love to create changes.

The Wind

The period between September 22 and October 22 is a time when the wind blows from the West, acting as a harbinger of transformation. The West Wind not only makes the leaves on trees fall to the ground, but it is also a symbol for introspection. In human terms, it means that the West Wind represents the middle years of life. This is a time when one takes stock and gets ready for more mature considerations.

Raven Character
Harmonious and peaceful interaction is very important for people born under the sign of the Raven, and that's why Ravens are often diplomatic and accommodating. They have a strong sense of fairness and justice. These qualities make them ideal mediators.

Being alone is particularly difficult for them. This accounts for the fact that they usually feel safe and more comfortable in groups and larger communities. They also dislike confrontations and would prefer to walk away from tricky situations than deal with them. Raven people always make an effort to see both sides of an issue and are masters in the deliberative processes. These traits, however, often keep them from making spontaneous decisions and forming opinions, which could mean missing important opportunities. In addition, Raven people have a tendency to be influenced by others.

People born under the sign of the Raven usually have a well-developed sense of beauty and aesthetics. It is not uncommon for them to have musical and artistic talents. They have a great need to be well-groomed and elegant, often concentrating too much on externals. They observe people and things very carefully, at least in terms of outward appearance, but sometimes fail to discover what's inside.

Love
Ravens seek out company and, therefore, need to have relationships more than people born under other signs. Turning to and showing devotion to a partner is an important key to their happiness. Charming and obliging as they are, they are masters of seduction, blessed in the art of living and loving. Flirting is a favorite preoccupation of Ravens.

Long live love and relationships! The single life was not invented by Ravens. They suffer a great deal when they have to live alone and will muster as much charm as they can to please and hold on to their partner and to avoid differences. In matters of the heart, Ravens give importance to all things relating to harmony and cooperation—even if they are totally submissive. They know what they want and have a great need for diversion and social connections.

Career Since Ravens are very cooperative and approachable, they rarely try to go it alone. They prefer working within a group or team. They are people who, to a great degree, contribute much to a comfortable working environment. But Ravens would do well, every now and then, to promote their own interests in a more spirited and energetic way. Because of their propensity toward the creative and beautiful things in life, they feel particularly comfortable where these criteria are met—such as in fashion, art, antiques, architecture, or engineering.

Vitality Ravens also should make sure they stay fit with consistent physical or athletic activities. Especially important are exercises that strengthen the back and pelvis, helping them stay in balance both physically and intellectually.

The Young Raven Even at a very young age, Ravens display a style and charm that is simply delightful. Generally speaking, these fledglings don't need to resort to temper tantrums or angry outbursts to get what they want. All they have to do is let people see their beaming smile. Since Ravens hate friction, regardless of age, they won't be much trouble to parents or teachers.

There are, however, some things that are difficult for the young Raven: making concrete and resolute decisions. It does not matter if the subject is homework or choosing what sweater to wear. The young Raven needs a lot of time for simple, everyday decisions. This can be nerve-racking for parents. They will do their child a great favor by giving simple, straight-forward directions, but not all the time. Young Ravens need to learn how to decide for themselves.

This also applies to the child's powerful need for peace, which leads him to avoid open confrontations. He will always try to be conciliatory, which, of course, does not always work. Sooner or later this child must learn that weighing both sides is not always possible. Sometimes it is necessary to stand up for one's own needs and interests. Young Ravens must learn not to say yes when they mean no.

The Raven and His or Her Partner

RAVEN AND FALCON

A Raven and Falcon relationship is likely to experience some conflict. While the elements fire and air complement each other, their personalities are very different. Harmony can be difficult to establish because the Falcon does not do well when it is time to compromise. Here the Raven will make more concessions than he would like, and frustration is likely.

RAVEN AND BEAVER

In the beginning, these two people won't have much in common. It might take a while for them to like each other. The Raven, influenced by the element fire, needs diversion, stimulation, and variety in his life, while Beaver is more inner-directed and loves domestic life.

RAVEN AND DEER

The element air is a good foundation for this combination. It both unites and heightens their relationship. Both signs take great joy in intellectual and social activities. Good communication and intense discourse is very important. While this relationship will not suffer from boredom, a calendar filled with too many different activities could be a source of stress. But—so what? Both Raven and Deer love it and feel connected because of it.

RAVEN AND WOODPECKER

It has been said that opposites attract, and this folk wisdom describes this relationship perfectly. But will Raven and Woodpecker get along? Not immediately. With goodwill and with time, a harmonious relationship can be established. However, this relationship will be made up of a lot of compromises.

RAVEN AND SALMON

Raven and Salmon can have a promising relationship because the elements fire and air usually go well together. Raven can lean on the strong Salmon (if Salmon allows him) and, in turn, Salmon enjoys Raven's social and cultivated life-style. In other words, their relationship is happy and harmonious.

RAVEN AND BROWN BEAR

Brown Bear has an even temperament and a steady nature. He loves rules he can depend on and favors safe boundaries and predictable schedules. It is possible that Raven will feel restricted in her natural tendencies. She cherishes diversion, loves not only being on the go but also the finer things in life. Misunderstandings are inevitable in such a relationship.

RAVEN AND RAVEN

Two Ravens will fly into each other arms. They belong to the element air and are in great need of varied and exciting stimulation, diversion, and entertainment. Since they perceive the world in much the same way, they will fulfill their desires effortlessly. The only thing this relationship may lack is emotional and spiritual depth. Their partnership may remain somewhat platonic and hinge on intellect rather than passion.

RAVEN AND SERPENT

Raven has a kind and accommodating personality and is always interested in balance. This often leads to having different opinions at different times, depending on the situation. Serpent, in comparison, tends to hold steadfast to an opinion once it has been reached. This could be a possible point of contention, particularly since, at times, Serpent wants to explore emotional aspects in more depth, something with which Raven is not comfortable.

RAVEN AND OWL

Since the elements fire and air are involved in this relationship, Raven and Owl get along well. They also have promising things in common that make for a very harmonious relationship. Among other things, it is particularly the diplomacy and tolerance of Raven that accommodates Owl's needs.

RAVEN AND GOOSE

When Raven and Goose meet, the spark of love might be missing in the beginning because of the difference in their personalities. The carefree attitude of Raven is difficult for Goose to understand because she lives life in moderation and has a serious and sober attitude. She could, however, learn a few things from Raven's carefree lifestyle. In turn, Raven could learn from concentration and consistency from Goose.

RAVEN AND OTTER

Whenever two people share the same element, things look very good indeed. Such is the relationship between Raven and Otter. The idealistic Otter, rich in ingenuity, can be very stimulating—something Raven seeks. Otter, on the other hand, finds in Raven a partner who will be interested in his plans and who supports them enthusiastically.

RAVEN AND WOLF

Raven and Wolf need time to respect and understand each other, if that is possible at all. Their greatest problem may be that Raven sometimes seems to be emotionally unavailable—which makes Wolf withdraw into his own world.

THE SERPENT

OCTOBER 23–NOVEMBER 22

Nature: *A Time of Death and Transformation*

Animal Totem: *Serpent*

Element: *Water*

Clan: *Frog*

Wind: *West Wind*

Strength: *Determination*

Weakness: *Rigidity*

The Animal Totem

In our culture Serpent is often viewed with repulsion, while in many other cultures she commands a great deal of respect. They view the Serpent as a symbol for transformation and renewal. This is possibly due to the animal's ability to shed its skin. The Serpent has also been seen as the protector of the mysteries of life who saved the secret wisdom from the reach of those who were not ready to receive it. Hypnotic, piercing eyes are typical for Serpent.

The Element

Serpent is influenced by the element water, which symbolizes deep emotions and unconscious, spiritual needs. Serpent people are keen observers and have the ability to recognize deep psychological undercurrents in other people.

The Clan

Serpent belongs to the Frog clan, which is also connected to the element water. Members of this clan are capable of very deep and intense emotions. Their strength is their good judgment and intuition. People can hide little from them. If they should try, Serpents will dig as long as it takes to find out what is going on. This makes them experts of the soul, who may not be well liked by everybody.

The Wind

During the period from October 23 to November 22 the wind blows from the West. The West Wind stirs us toward introspection and spirituality. The energies of life and nature do not push outward anymore but rather inward into the emotional and spiritual sphere. Hidden and secret matters want to be discovered and acknowledged. In this sense, Serpents are realistic.

Serpent Character

People born under the sign of the Serpent often have an entrancing gaze. They are enigmatic and unfathomable, which makes them fascinating as well as attractive and formidable. Serpents always want to know more than what their eyes can see. That accounts for the fact that many of them are explorers and researchers. However, they are not necessarily interested in scientific matters. They also delve into psychology, mysticism, and magic. They are particularly attracted to people and situations that are obscure, ambiguous, and dark. They eagerly dig into mysteries until they can solve them.

Serpents are also very competitive, determined, and persistent.. They pursue their goals vigorously and with logic. They never give up, even when they have reached their capacity, and sometimes they push beyond it. They are neither easy on themselves nor on others, which sometimes makes dealing with them difficult. On the other hand, one can count on their support when others have long since thrown in the towel.

Serpent people are true survivors, who often live between extremes. They can raise themselves to great heights but also fall into deep apathy. Others trust that they can set heaven and hell in motion. Their keen observations always allow them to get to the point.

Love

While Serpents are capable of very intense emotions and profound love, they also seem hesitant to reveal their love. This can be rather distressing for a partner, who must be patient and able to tolerate the ensuing tension until Serpent has gained trust and feels ready. When that happens, however, love can be most intense, even ecstatic.

Serpents are very reliable. They will go through thick and thin with a partner. The marriage vow "until death do us part" is taken literally. Like their animal totem, Serpents devour their love object skin and all—which is why some call them possessive and jealous. Indeed, this tendency is

not to be overlooked. Sometimes this can be burdensome and counter-productive, and eventually undermine the relationship. Serpents should practice more tolerance and learn to let go, so that love and passion do not turn into a source of frustration.

Career

Serpents pursue the goals of their profession and their work without reservation. They are very competitive, persistent, and usually quite competent. They are highly engaged and committed to their duties and tasks. Serpents are invaluable as co-workers or bosses because they can find the weaknesses in any system with a deadly accuracy as well as the remedies to deal with them.

In the heat of battle, Serpents often tend to resort to seemingly unfair methods. But they usually have good sense and enough expertise to make such action unnecessary. Serpents feel most comfortable in research positions.

Vitality

Sometimes Serpents control their emotions so much that it robs them of their vitality. This often affects the stomach and digestive system, particularly when stress is involved. People born under the sign of the Serpent should let their energies flow readily and freely to avoid blockages that can, among other things, cause them to become aggressive.

The Young Serpent

Young Serpents develop a strong personality early. This child is active, interested, and eager to learn. He starts to discover life and test boundaries very early. He also begins early to experiment with toys, self, and with his parents. This demands that his parents have a great deal of child-rearing know-how. It also presents certain dangers. Knives, forks, scissors, candles, and matches should be out of reach until the child is mature and sensible enough to use them responsibly.

School and learning usually are a real joy for Serpent children because they help satisfy his curiosity. But teachers will often be caught short because of this child's probing questions. Serpent children are interested in more than the ABC's or $1 + 1 = 2$. In the face of unfairness, young Serpents quickly show an active and energetic side and fight not only for themselves but also for other students, correcting what they believe to be wrong. The result is that young Serpents are often elected to be leaders of their peers, like class president.

This child certainly is self-sufficient and able to cope with life. He will find his way. However, difficulties arise when puberty begins and sexuality becomes a factor. Adolescent Serpents may explore these new dynamics all too precociously and intensely. That's why it is important for young Serpents to deal with these early experiences carefully.

The Serpent and His or Her Partner

SERPENT AND FALCON

Serpent is a person with deep and passionate emotions. Inside the Falcon also burns a bright fire with strong emotions and great passion. While this may at first look like a perfect union, there is a fly in the soup. The emotions of Serpent are held deep within the soul, and those of the Falcon are expressed more outwardly and spontaneously. Sparks will fly.

SERPENT AND BEAVER

Serpent and Beaver constitute two opposing poles, which can give both a chance to meet in the middle and forge an enviable unit. But doing so is not all that easy. The opposing tendencies and needs require a high degree of tolerance and acceptance.

SERPENT AND DEER

The emotional Serpent would love nothing more than to snag the emotional side of Deer and claim him for her own. But Stag will resist any pressure quickly and skillfully. This will leave a drop of bitterness: that of unrequited love. Over the long haul, neither partner will be satisfied.

SERPENT AND WOODPECKER

Since Woodpecker, like Serpent, belongs to the element water, neither will find it difficult to forge an intimate relationship, particularly since theirs rests on a strong emotional foundation. Serpent and Woodpecker, who find in each other everything they have searched for, will never let go.

SERPENT AND SALMON

Whenever the elements water and fire meet, one must be prepared for a few difficulties and misunderstandings. With the proud and domineering Salmon and the ruthlessly honest Serpent, friction is almost guaranteed. Both tend to be jealous and possessive, so finding a solution to any difficulties is hard for them.

SERPENT AND BROWN BEAR

The above scenario does not occur when Serpent meets Brown Bear. The latter is accommodating, undemanding, and able to appreciate the Serpent's sensitivity, steadfastness, and dependability. The fact that Brown Bear carefully holds back many of his deepest feelings could invigorate the relationship, because Serpent thrives on challenges—especially emotional ones.

SERPENT AND RAVEN

Corresponding to the element water, Serpents' emotions are as deep as the ocean, and they love to pull their partner down into the very emotional depths they experience. Ravens, however, do not always feel very comfortable in that sphere (they fear drowning) and will, to a great degree, hold back emotionally. It will be difficult, even impossible, to create a fulfilling relationship.

SERPENT AND SERPENT

Two Serpents could fall under each other's spell—physically, emotionally, and intellectually. Their profound connection may well be for life. Their emotions can be so deep that they are sometimes painful. Their intensity and passion are enviable. But such strong passions and the tendency to be jealous can also cause problems.

SERPENT AND OWL

Serpents and Owls are unlikely to fall immediately into each other's arms, even though Owls are by nature spontaneous and euphoric. But contradictions within such relationships do exist, and in the beginning, these contradictions may stand in the way of happiness. If, however, Serpent is

able to be less possessive, and if Owl exercises the tolerance that she is capable of, nothing will stand in the way of forging a constructive and intense relationship.

SERPENT AND GOOSE
Serpent and Goose love to get to know each other because they are both drawn by the water element, though Goose is governed by earth. While both have a tendency to control their deeper feelings, the sensual and passionate flame that burns between them will strengthen and deepen their relationship. A union between Serpent and Goose promises to be very successful—in love and at work.

SERPENT AND OTTER
Serpent is influenced by the element water, and Otter is influenced by the element air. So, the two approach each other with mixed feelings because they live in such different worlds. Great tolerance might be required from both, perhaps more than they are able to give.

SERPENT AND WOLF
The sensitive and accommodating Wolf might just hit the bull's-eye with Serpent, and vice versa. Both belong to the element water, and both live in such rich emotional worlds that their shared emotional depth guarantees a strong foundation and an indestructible bond. In addition, Wolf will quickly win Serpent's trust.

THE OWL

NOVEMBER 23–DECEMBER 21

Nature: *A Time of Hibernation*

Animal Totem: *Owl*

Element: *Fire*

Clan: *Hawk*

Wind: *West Wind*

Strengths: *Idealism, Wisdom*

Weaknesses: *Being Overbearing, Restlessness*

The Animal Totem

Owl is a creature of the night. In ancient cultures this imposing bird was the symbol for wisdom and knowledge. A keen observer, with sharp and alert eyes, the Owl operates and catches her prey in darkness. She has uncanny accuracy and misses nothing. Sometimes the Owl gives the impression of being bored and indifferent, sometimes interested and wise, as though she were above all worldly things.

The Element

Owl people are influenced by the element fire, an element symbolizing spontaneity, enthusiasm, and idealism. However, in Owls, fire does not burn wildly and uncontrolled. It glows quietly and softly. The power of fire is used to acquire spiritual knowledge.

The Clan

Owl belongs to the Hawk clan, which makes Owl people levelheaded and farsighted. They strive for deeper understanding. The driving force behind them is a quiet and lasting inner fire. In order to acquire more knowledge, members of the Hawk clan, and particularly Owl, are willing to pursue any adventure or challenge that life offers. Owls grow and mature with their tasks.

The Wind

During the time between November 23 and December 21 the wind blows from the West. This is a time of long nights and introspection. Nature also pulls back, preparing for the long winter. But nature's stillness only affects things on the surface. Hidden underground, inside trees, and below the snow, much is happening. In nature as well as in the human soul, this is when new ideas are born from nights dark and obscure.

Owl Character

With the element fire, Owl people have an enduring strength that allows them to follow their high ideals and formidable goals. This is why people often think of them as haughty and arrogant. That does not bother Owl people. They know that there is more between heaven and earth than logic and materialism. They strive for a deeper understanding and a more profound truth.

This is why Owl can be so committed to her ideals. She has plenty of enthusiasm and little difficulty inspiring others. She has great difficulty tolerating narrow-mindedness and restrictions. Owl people need a lot of freedom and independence to pursue their goals. After all, the world is a place much in need of improvement. A missionary zeal is not uncommon among Owls, and sometimes they overdo it and appear to be know-it-alls.

In any case, Owls love a good debate because during intense conversations ideas can be exchanged and new insights and attitudes developed. Generally speaking, Owls are open and very direct, sometimes to the point of tactlessness. Owls must learn to accept different opinions and ideas.

Love

Owls are adventurous and excited about life in general and love in particular. They need an intellectual and emotional dialogue. Owls love to flirt, engaging the opposite sex in intense conversations for no other reason than to test that person's attitude. If a spark is ignited, passion is not far behind. The intimate life with an Owl partner is exciting and adventurous.

However, people born under the sign of the Owl are slow to make a commitment. That would mean loss of their freedom and independence—something quite frightening for Owls. As in the case of Falcon or Salmon, it is important that love and relationships do not lose their attrac-

tion. Once the dynamics in a relationship become routine, Owl may wander. And a new flirtation often leads to new adventures. Owl's partner must remain interesting and stimulating. Of course, that's easier said than done.

Career People born under the sign of the Owl have many talents and can work successfully in many professions. The most important criteria for a satisfying and fulfilling career, however, are that they can work independently and have decision-making power. Owls are unable to thrive in subordinate positions. In addition, they are not very good at taking and carrying out orders without being able to analyze them.

Thanks to their power of persuasion, they make very good salespeople and publishers. But they also do well as lawyers, law clerks, and judges. Owls delight in teaching in universities, and many become theologians or clerics and politicians intent on creating a better world. These professions draw Owls because knowledge—or better yet wisdom—and reforming the world remain very close to their heart.

Vitality For Owls the most vulnerable physical areas are the hips, thighs, and ankle joints, which are more sensitive than for people born under other signs. They would do well to avoid overexertion, particularly in athletic activities.

Owls have a penchant for food and drink, which may lead to weight gain and liver problems. Since they always draw on seemingly unlimited resources, moderation does not come easily to them. But for the sake of their health they should exercise more discipline, controlling what and how much they eat and drink.

The Young Owl
Young Owls are energetic, enterprising, social but-terflies. Full of life, they have a refreshing, positive attitude that puts every-body around them in a good mood. They are a delight for parents, pro-vided that they treat their young Owls as equal partners. However, Owls can also be very demanding. Unlike many other children, they are espe-cially curious and often ask: "Why?" or "How come?" Sometimes par-ents are hard put to find plausible answers or explanations. If the reply is not believable, heaven help them! Young Owls can be very indignant.

This highly energetic and active child needs a lot of space for playing and romping about, and parents would do well to channel some of the young Owl's energy into sports-related activities. In addition, this child needs to be able to be outside, where he can have a chance to use his adventurous spirit to explore and discover the world. If possible, parents should provide a pet. Owl children are caring and devoted animal lovers.

In general, young Owls love to learn, provided that the subject is inter-esting and the teacher not boring. They love activities with other children in small groups and usually appoint themselves, in a pleasant way, the leader. Owls are full of ideas and suggestions. Young Owls mature rela-tively early and are well able to stand on their own two feet.

The Owl and His or Her Partner

OWL AND FALCON

The element fire rules this relationship. This means that not only is there good cooperation between both, but that Owl and Falcon have a spontaneous and genuine exchange of feelings. One is almost tempted to declare them a dream couple. They enrich each other, and together they can do almost anything to which they set their minds. Falcon gladly supports Owl's idealistic endeavors.

OWL AND BEAVER

Owl and Beaver do not always get along. When steadfast and deliberate Beaver meets Owl, Owl often feels restricted. Beaver often finds it difficulty to understand Owl's bold and idealistic dreams. This is reason enough for them not to rush to the altar too fast.

OWL AND DEER

Initially, Owl and Deer will like each other, since fire and air, their respective elements, complement each other. Both seek knowledge, activity, and sociability. But on closer inspection, a few contradictions, which can only be overcome with tolerance and much hard work, will be apparent. Owl should try to be less exacting, and Deer should try to approach things more seriously.

OWL AND WOODPECKER

Owl and Woodpecker have a few differences to overcome if they choose to be a couple. An important requirement to a lasting relationship is goodwill. Woodpecker often prefers to keep Owl home, which she won't like at all. If Owl's freedom and independence are seriously restricted, she will take off.

OWL AND SALMON

Both Owl and Salmon belong to the element fire. A harmless flirtation could quickly turn serious, as long as Salmon, in his generosity and openness, can bring himself to understand the idealism and flights of fancy typical for Owl. Furthermore, if Salmon keeps his jealous streak in check, nothing will stand in the way of a passionate and enduring love realtionship.

OWL AND BROWN BEAR

Brown Bear and Owl's relationship is unlikely to be passionate and enduring. Brown Bear relies more on facts than fancies, and Owl spends his life searching for truth and questioning reality. Only if both are able to understand the interests and views of the other can this relationship grow.

OWL AND RAVEN

Owl and Raven can be a good team, which is as interesting as it is spirited. Since Raven is intellectually open and able to see things and ideas realistically, he can act as a motivator as well as an advisor. Also, Owl's entrepreneurial spirit and Raven's sense of adventure are promising criteria for happiness and harmony.

OWL AND SERPENT

Fire and water are elements that do not go together. Owl seeks high ideals and is attracted by intellectual pursuits. Serpent, on the other hand, is more at home in the deep and mysterious world of the soul. Misunderstandings won't be long in coming. Both are willing explorers, and this could help bridge the different worlds in which they live.

OWL AND OWL

Two Owls together! What an exciting and fascinating relationship this could be, ruled by the element fire. A double dose of idealism and

engagement can propel this pair. They are also unbeatable when it comes to making plans. Ideally, each will pay attention to the needs of the other and thereby maintain a happy love relationship.

Owl and Goose

Here Owl will probably bang his head against a brick wall. The sensible, realistic, and disciplined Goose will bring Owl back to the hard facts of reality. The result usually is frustrating. But if Owl is able to be convincing, Goose will provide an unconditional and reliable support.

Owl and Otter

Owl and Otter like each other immediately. Both are made for love-at-first-sight. Both are very competitive, each trying to come up with the best idea, the most outrageous adventure, and the most humanitarian views. Theirs will be a relationship in which both partners positively influence the other's personal development.

Owl and Wolf

This combination is likely to be burdened with many difficulties. The elements water and fire require that both Owl and Wolf work hard at their relationship. The question is: Are they both willing to make the effort? At best, this will be a relationship based on tolerance and acceptance and that may not be enough for both.

THE GOOSE

DECEMBER 22–JANUARY 19

Nature: A Time of Renewal

Animal Totem: Goose

Element: Earth

Clan: Turtle

Wind: North Wind

Strength: Perseverance

Weaknesses: Rigidity, Mistrust

The Animal Totem While there are many different Goose species, the Snow Goose usually represents this animal totem. The Canada Goose is also a popular representative. Like most Geese, the Snow Goose is a good swimmer who also appears comfortable on land, where she finds her food. The Snow Goose flies in huge flocks, often covering thousands of miles or kilometers in migration from the Arctic. She leaves her northern nesting grounds with the earliest snowfall and returns after the snow melts. This behavior is a sign of her versatility, tenacity, and focused energy.

The Element Goose is influenced by the element earth, which stands for steadfastness and stability. In addition, people born under this totem have a healthy dose of competitiveness and perseverance. Guided by the motto "In silence lies strength," people born under the sign of the Goose have big plans and, by climbing steadily, go far.

The Clan Goose is a member of the earthbound Turtle clan. Members of this clan have a particular need for secure and stabile surroundings. They usually know exactly what they want and what they have to do to reach the goals they set for themselves. They are reliable and have an ambition, perseverance, and steadiness that are admirable. But concentrating so hard on a task often diminishes their flexibility.

The Wind During the period between December 22 and January 19, the wind blows from the North. The bitter cold forces nature—plants, animals, and people—to rest. This is also the time just after the winter solstice, with the shortest day and longest night of the year. Everything appears frozen and lifeless. But soon the days begin to grow longer, light will resume its fight against darkness, and light will again prevail.

Goose Character

People born under the sign of the Goose are strong. This strength does not express itself in hasty decisions or exaggerated, spontaneous actions. Even when very busy, Geese take the time to rationally consider their action. While they usually set their sights high, they try to be realistic and sensible and to pursue their goals with enviable persistence and remarkable ambition.

Such a focused and serious attitude toward life often leads others to judge them as distant and even cold. But that is only marginally correct. Geese simply react more calmly. They tend to be more restrained so that they avoid disappointments. Under their rough exterior, however, beats a rather soft heart.

Since Geese prefer quality above quantity, they have a tendency to separate the wheat from the chaff in both professional and social life. Remarkable also is the vitality of Geese. They seem to have unlimited energy, allowing them to work nonstop. When others are close to collapse, they get ready to roll up their sleeves. However, this competitive drive and strong sense of responsibility may make them miss, even deny themselves, the more beautiful and pleasant side of life. This often is due simply to too much modesty and self-restraint.

Love

Those who are looking for a faithful, reliable person, who offers 100 percent, no one could do no better than to choose a Goose or Gander. Geese take love as seriously as they do their work and responsibilities. It might, however, take a while until they open up emotionally and show the deep feelings of which they are capable. Geese need time to build the trust that is necessary for a fulfilling permanent relationship.

But when they do build that trust, Geese will be caring and loving partners. Geese not only offer security and safety, but they also bring a good measure of passion and seductive sensuality to everyday life.

Sometimes Geese lack imagination. After all, they are realistic and practical people. For that reason, it won't hurt if the partner can provide stimulating activities and diversion every now and then, not only in everyday life but also in their love life. Goose and Gander will surely fall for those suggestions, even if in a restrained manner.

Career

People born under the sign of the Goose are ambitious, expert planners who know how to figure things out. They do not leave professional development to chance. On the contrary, responsible goals are established relatively early. Geese will not rest until their goals have been reached, even if it should take years. Geese start from the bottom up. While that takes time, it has the advantage that they know their subject matter, and nobody can fool them or hold a candle to them. A survey of managers and bosses would reveal that many of them are born under the sign of the Goose.

Vitality

Geese are vibrant and physically fit. Since they have the talent to use their energy and time well, they are deliberate and determined. They also have very few health problems. Furthermore, they don't give in easily. Little discomforts are often ignored or worked through. But Gander and Goose both need to be careful to avoid overexertion and exhaustion. The most sensitive organ of Geese is the skin. It becomes irritated and prone to allergies when Geese suppress their feelings. Many Geese also have unstable knees.

The Young Goose Young Goose or Gander is rather subdued and sometimes even shy. This child will never seek the limelight. He appears to be happy with what he has or what his parents provide and loves to entertain himself. He is a thoughtful and serious child. Ambition and a sense of responsibility, characteristic of the person born under the sign of the Goose, starts to develop early. For parents who have to deal with a lot of stress, a Gosling is a true blessing. For that reason, parents need to make sure that the child has a chance to really be a child and not a small adult.

Sometimes, Goslings are too serious. They need to learn that life also has a fun and light side. Otherwise, the intensity of their activities can keep them house-bound, allowing too little contact with children their own age and too little physical activity. The tendency to be a loner begins to show itself early in life. Parents need to encourage social interaction.

The young Goose and Gander is industrious, ambitious, and has few problems in school. Good efforts and correspondingly good grades are a given. That notwithstanding, the young Goose may still suffer from a lack of self-esteem. It is, therefore, essential to praise him frequently, but honestly, so that the child knows and learns to enjoy success. Parents should not let him walk through life with blinders. He needs to be encouraged to play, have fun, and be physically active. Young Goslings, like grown-up Geese, make loyal friends.

The Goose and His or Her Partner

GOOSE AND FALCON

Goose and Falcon won't get too upset with each other quickly. Goose will simply be astounded when she is watching the daring, spontaneous, and sometimes not-well-thought-out activities of Falcon. In turn Falcon, given his intense and stormy emotions, will have difficulty understanding the self-controlled Goose. These two will certainly need a lot of patience and forbearance if they want to forge a good relationship.

GOOSE AND BEAVER

Since Goose and Beaver are both influenced by the element earth, they have very similar opinions and needs. Both are faithful and reliable partners who can give much to each other. Happily, Beaver is an expert in the art of living and will make sure that the ambitious, responsible, and hard-working Gander finds needed diversions.

GOOSE AND DEER

Just as quickly as the nimble Doe or Stag appears, he may also be gone again. Influenced by the element air, Deer are driven from one activity to another, something the earth-bound Goose or Gander can't really understand. Both Goose and Gander hate undependable people, particularly in matters of love. These two will have great difficulty making the relationship work.

GOOSE AND WOODPECKER

Since the elements earth and water are involved, a certain attraction is a given. But needs, interests, and tendencies may still run in different directions. Goose controls feelings, often to the point of appearing cool, while the sensitive Woodpecker positively dissolves with passionate emotions. But a wonderful relationship is possible if both are willing to compromise.

GOOSE AND SALMON

Among other things, Goose is known for being thrifty. Salmon, on the other hand, flows over with generosity, in material as well as emotional arenas. Maybe Goose, under the affectionate influence of Salmon, could be persuaded to be a bit more spontaneous. She would not regret it! Goose and Salmon do have a few qualities in common: ambition, determination, and assertiveness.

GOOSE AND BROWN BEAR

Goose and Brown Bear seem to be made for each other. The influence of the element earth, which both share, has a stabilizing and unifying effect on this promising relationship. But this is also a relationship of two frugal and modest people. They may stay together under a notion of duty and obligation rather than a feeling of pleasure. They both need to make sure they do not relegate pleasure to the back burner in their relationship.

GOOSE AND RAVEN

Raven has many interests, behaves diplomatically, has an active intellect and, most of all, charm. The question is, however, whether this relationship can engage Gander over the long haul. Being influenced by earth, Gander expects a certain amount of stability. But stability is not something Raven can offer him.

GOOSE AND SERPENT

With Serpent, Goose could have found a real treasure. Serpent is sensitive and able to understand what motivates Goose. There are several characteristics these two have in common, so that the relationship seems to run under its own power. The magical and passionate aura of Serpent may just be what is needed to lure Goose out of her reserve.

GOOSE AND OWL

It will take some time until earth and fire can nourish each other, but nothing is impossible. Once a small spark of tenderness has been ignited between the two, both will try to understand each other. However, this does not mean that both share the same view about things. Much work is needed to achieve a viable relationship.

GOOSE AND GANDER

It is obvious that when Goose meets Gander basic questions about life and love need no discussion. The element they share, earth, made sure of that. If viewed from this perspective, the chances for a long and fulfilling relationship are very good. To bring excitement into the relationship, it would be good if both are not too serious and make room for fun and pleasure. Otherwise, love could quickly become a matter of routine, and boredom will knock at the door.

GOOSE AND OTTER

Goose needs reliability in everything, particularly when it comes to a partner. This is something Otter cannot guarantee. He is very impulsive, which does not always make him a reliable person. That is difficult for Goose to tolerate. Such differences make for a very unequal relationship.

GOOSE AND WOLF

While at first the realistic and practical Gander won't understand the romantic and hidden desires and needs of Wolf, these two could perfectly complement each other. Gander only needs to let go of his skepticism and learn to trust Wolf's instinctive and intuitive talents.

THE OTTER

JANUARY 20–FEBRUARY 18

Nature: *A Time of Preparation*

Animal Totem: *Otter*

Element: *Air*

Clan: *Butterfly*

Wind: *North Wind*

Strengths: *Creativity, Humor*

Weaknesses: *Volatility, Rebelliousness*

The Animal Totem
Otters are quick and agile. They belong to the weasel family and are built to move on land as well as in the water. Watching them is a sheer delight. They are playful and boisterous animals. Particularly fascinating is how skillfully they move, given the fact that they are compact and almost 4 feet or over 1 meter long. The mischief they usually get into is very appealing. They like to slide on the belly down snowbanks.

The Element
Otters are influenced by the element air, which accounts for their flexibility, intelligence, communication, and wealth of ideas. Air also helps Otters to understand the connection that we have to the environment. It is reasonable to assume that someone born under this sign is always ready to provide intellectual stimulation.

The Clan
Otters belong to the Butterfly clan, which explains their free spirit and verbal skill. On the other hand, Otters also have a tendency to waste their energies because they seem to weigh every possibility and often lose sight of essentials.

The Wind
During the period between January 20 and February 18 the wind blows from the North. The ground is still frozen, and the blanket of snow can seem to paralyze some activity. But underneath, something apparently dormant maintains its vitality. It is obvious that the power and influence of the Sun is increasing. While new life, waiting for the new cycle of the season, is still hidden, the promise and hope of renewal is invigorating and motivating.

Otter Character
Knowing intuitively that nature will soon bring forth new and splendid life, people born under the sign of the Otter also are full of hope and confidence. They are active (particularly intellectually), well-liked, and altruistic people. In addition, they are blessed with a wonderful sense of humor. Since they have a very keen sense of justice, Otters cannot tolerate the fact that very privileged people exist side-by-side with people who are poor. Otters are revolutionaries and rebels.

Individuality aside, Otters are still very cooperative and capable of positively influencing the team spirit in groups and organizations. Friendship and solidarity are very important for Otters. They will share or even give away their last shirt when a friend is in need or someone is helpless and needs support. They are also very sociable people who in company are often the life of the party.

People born under the sign of the Otter love to support positive changes and progress in society at large, and they usually have very interesting ideas. Some of those ideas may be truly utopian, with very little chance of being put into practice.

Love
When it comes to love, it is worth mentioning that, just as in the case of Owls, Otters are very particular about their personal freedom and independence. They expect their partner to respect that need, and they are tolerant enough to grant the same in return. While they view sexuality as part of a pleasant intimate relationship, for Otters sex is not the first priority. Intellectual compatibility is much more important.

People who want to build and maintain a happy relationship need to know how to keep loose reins. In return, Otters make sure nothing becomes routine. Boredom will not intrude. They love diversion and surprises. In this way, Otters, influenced by the element air, can always be counted on to keep love fresh and new—provided they believe that they are doing it of their own free will.

Career

People born under the sign of the Otter could never work in civil service, not even in the higher ranks. In order to express their creative and intellectual talents, these witty, pioneering, and independent people need a lot of elbow room and personal freedom, even in their working environment.

Since Otters have so many talents, it is not important what kind of work they do. Much more important is that they work independently and are given serious responsibilities. They have a great deal of difficulty with orders from above. They do not deal well with authority. As children, many Otters probably wanted to be astronauts or explorers.

Vitality

Full of intellectual ideas, Otters have high expectations of themselves and of people in general. Occasionally, this creates stress, particularly if they have not learned to take a break and relax, not from physical but from mental activities.

From a physical point of view, Otters seldom overtax themselves. They know how to use their energies. Sometimes they even tend to be apathetic. They may occasionally experience difficulty with the heart and circulatory system. But with regular exercise, Otters can remain subtle and fit into old age.

The Young Otter

Young Otters are very alert and interested children who begin asking "Why?" relatively early. Parents are often challenged. Most of all, these children want to be treated as partners, having a well-developed sense of fairness early and believing in equal rights for all. The question of age is of no interest to them.

Young Otters begin early to analyze the family structure and to rearrange it. At least they will try! This child believes that he is competent to improve the quality of his life as well as those of others. He will take apart things that have already been tested and proven to work, and he will suggest changes. While that may appear funny at times, it can also be stressful. His early improvements may not have been well thought out. The task of Otter's parents is to teach this resourceful child the art of compromise.

In school, too, young Otters do not take everything as a given. While good and quick learners, Otters are much more interested in what is not taught. They are always interested in things that they believe can be improved. Otter's friendly personality also becomes apparent early on. Nothing makes him happier than having his classmates around him, and he chooses that as often as possible. Before his parents know what is happening, they discover that their home has a revolving front door with people coming and going. But they need not worry. Their child has interesting friends, and the family may profit from the fresh air the young Otter brings into the house.

The Otter and His or Her Partner

OTTER AND FALCON

The elements air and fire in this relationship will prove to be stimulating and refreshing. Both will quickly be smitten with each other, and what was just a little flirtation may soon turn into something serious. However, it would be prudent for the passionate Falcon to tone down his feelings, saving some of his energy for a more intellectual exchange with Otter.

OTTER AND BEAVER

Otter and Beaver need to take care of a few differences before they can hope to have a satisfying relationship. This is a relationship between an idealist and a materialist. Both positions have their place. But to make this relationship work, they have to compromise. Are the compromises they have to make too numerous?

OTTER AND DEER

Both Otter and Deer, influenced by the element air, are restless and chafing at the bit. They could stimulate and positively influence each other. Since both are active and adventurous, they would rather be living with chronic scheduling stress than in a routine everyday existence. The latter will create problems much more quickly. This couple will be constantly on the go.

OTTER AND WOODPECKER

Woodpecker, given her dependency and need for security, will most likely try to interfere with Otter's cherished need for freedom. At worst, this relationship will not survive. Otter, as soon as he senses that his independence is in serious danger, will take off in a hurry, even if this means leaving behind a heartbroken Woodpecker.

OTTER AND SALMON

Otter and Salmon, what a tension-filled relationship! Although air and fire, usually harmonize, their other characteristics are diametrically opposed. However, this can be stimulating as well as stressful for a partnership. On the positive side, both can learn from and with each other under one condition: that both are willing and gracious enough to make concessions. This, of course, means that both must compromise—Otter, her ideals and Salmon, his ego.

OTTER AND BROWN BEAR

Neither will fall down on his or her knees as soon as they meet. Otter, influenced by the element air, needs time to get used to earth-bound Brown Bear, particularly when Bear gets petty, persnickety, and a little intolerant. But one thing unites Otter and Brown Bear: in their own way, both are intellectually interesting, nimble, and open-minded.

OTTER AND RAVEN

Air influences both signs or partners. This allows Otter and Raven to create and support a harmonious and uncomplicated relationship. While Otter's strong idealistic engagement is not always to Raven's liking, Otter can certainly contribute intellectual stimulation. Moreover, many of their activities will enrich this relationship.

OTTER AND SERPENT

Otter and Serpent will often be on a warpath, and seemingly incompatible differences will make it difficult for this relationship to succeed. Serpent has a tendency to want her partner all to herself. Otter sees red and quickly disappears. If he stays, the relationship will contain never-ending compromises, and that does not bode well for a long-lasting relationship.

OTTER AND OWL

Otter and Owl are not only connected by the elements air and fire, they also complement each other in their idealism and desire for truth. These two signs encourage each other. Otter and Owl are mutually stimulating in all areas of life. This relationship deserves the adjective *precious*.

OTTER AND GOOSE

In this relationship the road to happiness is paved with many obstacles, but they can be overcome. However, Goose is very disciplined and she may try to counter Otter's idealism with reason. The result would be a relationship built on compromise and trust.

OTTER AND OTTER

Two Otters can frolic together. They can improve each other and the whole world. They both share the element air, which promotes intellectual energy and openness. This does, however, push emotional issues to second place and encourages a certain amount of superficiality. That, however, is not a problem if both partners are satisfied.

OTTER AND WOLF

When taking a close look, Otter and Wolf are strangers. Both approach life from different sides. Otter, however, is always open to differing views. Wolf, thanks to his sensitivity, can empathize with others. Both might be able to find common ground. The keys are Otter's broad intuitive sense and Wolf's fine instincts.

THE WOLF

FEBRUARY 19–MARCH 20

Nature: *A Time of Renewal*

Animal Totem: *Wolf*

Element: *Water*

Clan: *Frog*

Wind: *North Wind*

Strength: *Sensitivity*

Weaknesses: *Laziness, Easily Influenced*

The Animal Totem
Even though Wolf appears to be very powerful, he is also anxious and extremely cautious, at least when away from the pack. However, he usually travels with a pack. Unlike his close relatives, Fox and Coyote, known for their wiliness, he is able to live within a community, which makes hunting for food easier. A pack can handle larger prey. While the expression on Wolf's face often seems to indicate mistrust, it also displays loyalty. Wolves are indeed very loyal. A Wolf pair stays together for life.

The Element
Wolf is influenced by the element water, which stands for feelings, sensitivity, and empathy. People influenced by the element water can also be tossed about by their emotions. They need to work on finding stability and balance.

The Clan
Wolf belongs to the Frog clan. Members of this clan, due to their deep feelings and the ability to be empathetic, are able to identify with other people and their needs. They are sympathetic and supportive. On the other hand, they are also in danger of becoming too dependent on the emotional support of others.

The Wind
During the period between February 19 and March 20, the wind blows from the North, a direction that symbolizes purity and cleansing. The experiences and wisdom gathered throughout the cycle of nature, starting with the Falcon period, now comes together and gives us a hint of what is to come. Nature prepares for renewal, the beginning of a new cycle. That makes this a time of anticipation and premonition.

Wolf Character

People born under the sign of the Wolf are very sensitive. They seem to have a special antenna for what is happening around them. It is fascinating how they seem to know what other people need without anybody having to say a word. This degree of sensitivity can, however, also be misunderstood, prompting Wolf people to withhold their most intense feelings.

Even though Wolf is a pack animal, people born under this animal totem also need their solitude. They often retreat to a quiet and peaceful place because of the need to be alone with their dreams. These sensitive people depend on their fantasies to escape the harshness of the world from time to time. Since intuition and instinct are their hallmark, Wolves have a remarkable knowledge of human nature. It is also not unusual to find them interested in all things mystical. Indeed, they know or perceive more of the secrets of life than many of their contemporaries.

Wolves are helpful, empathetic, and devoted. But they can also be somewhat gullible, often resulting in their good-natured support being misused. In order to protect himself, Wolf subconsciously has a tendency to isolate himself. For this reason Wolf must have a private, quiet place where he can recharge his batteries. He intensely dislikes it when people intrude on this place, uninvited.

Love

Wolves are made for romantic love and devotion. They will be totally dedicated to their mate because they instinctively know what makes her happy. They will leave no stone unturned to fulfill their partner's every desire. In spite of the deep and intense feelings of which Wolf is capable, he will not give away his heart carelessly. When he gives his heart, he does so for life. He will wait patiently for a long time, until the right person comes along.

People born under the sign of the Wolf need a lot of tenderness.

Passion alone does less than a heartfelt embrace. They are receptive and grateful for a friendly word. However, they idolize their partner, often so much that the partner feels overwhelmed. How can one do justice to an exaggerated ideal? This can easily lead to problems. Another source of irritation is that Wolf needs his little secrets. A partner may easily feel left out. But not to worry! Wolf is faithful and deserves absolute trust.

Career

Since Wolf is not the most ambitious person and does not mind going with the flow, he will never rise rapidly in the working world or in his profession. Wolves watch how things are developing and decide, instinctively, what needs to be done. In this gentle and wonderful way the Wolf will, slowly but surely, reach a position others tried to get with dogged determination.

Wolves are helpful and empathetic. They don't only want to do well for themselves but want the same for everybody else. This might be the reason many Wolf people can be found in the service sector and in healing and creative professions. With great devotion Wolves are committed to helping those less fortunate. But they are also attracted to the arts.

Vitality

One way for Wolves to escape the harsh realities of the world is to indulge in imagination and fantasy. Such a tendency could, however, lead to the use of addictive substances, which could allow them, for a little while at least, to see the world through rose-colored glasses. That's why it is important that Wolfves exercise discipline and become aware of the consequences of their habits. They also would profit from checking their eating habits. Countering frustration with sweets will eventually lead to weight problems. Other than that, Wolves often have to deal with foot problems. They should take good care of their feet and remember to elevate them often.

The Young Wolf
Young Wolves are gentle and loving children. Parents might sometimes ask themselves if everything is okay. These little kids doe not seem to know what a temper tantrums or angry outburst is. But Wolf pups still get what they want with a look and a magic smile rather than by screaming. Adults will simply melt.

Wolf has a rich imagination and is particularly fond of fairy tales and mysteries. He could listen for hours, seemingly disappearing into a world filled with magic. Since the young Wolf pup is very sensitive, he does not always have enough self-confidence to assert himself. He needs a lot of attention, patience, and encouragement to be more bold. This is true for everyday, practical situations but especially when he is in school or in training.

Parents and teachers need to be very careful and gentle when it comes to teaching the sensitive Wolf discipline. He has a tendency to withdraw from strenuous subjects, seeking refuge in his dreams. He is not very consistent in matters of work because he is very much ruled by his emotions. However, once a subject has caught his fancy, he becomes intensely devoted to it and gives it his full attention. Since the young Wolf is very clinging and compassionate, he will try to remain in his idyllic home as long as possible. But even after he has left, he will always stay in close touch with his parents and the old neighborhood.

The Wolf and His or Her Partner

WOLF AND FALCON

Falcon will try to conquer Wolf with passion and, possibly, fall flat on his face. Wolf is sensitive and compassionate, and she knows how to protect herself against uninvited advances. Falcon has two choices: he can either tone down his passionate foray or admit defeat.

WOLF AND BEAVER

Beaver can surely make the heart of Wolf beat faster! Wolf, influenced by the element water, would love to lean on the quiet, steadfast Beaver. But Beaver should not be too sure of herself. She should be ready to acknowledge and reciprocate the sensitive signals Wolf is sending, which, of course, is not an easy task! If she fails, the emotional potential will remain unfulfilled.

WOLF AND DEER

In this relationship it is possible that both partners will talk and "live" beyond the reach of each other. The worlds Wolf and Deer live in are different. But there is one chance: if Wolf will activate his compassion, and Doe her intellectual imagination. This is how they could slowly and carefully get to know and understand each other.

WOLF AND WOODPECKER

Wolf and Woodpecker are both influenced by the element water. They could really be a dream couple. One look and they know that here is the perfect emotional foundation for a lasting union. Even small misunderstandings and differences, which are bound to happen during everyday life, won't seriously threaten the tranquility in their relationship.

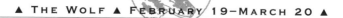
WOLF AND SALMON

Salmon shines with his strong, dynamic, and heartwarming personality. That could be an invitation for Wolf to depend on and be protected by him. The fact that Salmon needs to set the tone is of little concern to Wolf. But if Salmon is not ready to become more deeply involved emotionally, the relationship will always be bitter-sweet.

WOLF AND BROWN BEAR

In principle, the elements water and earth are not in conflict, but Wolf and Brown Bear are. Their interests, needs, and development go in different directions, and the balancing influence of the elements cannot bridge this gap. In this relationship it is the head and the heart that need to be united. How lucky that Wolf is compassionate and Brown Bear willing to learn.

WOLF AND RAVEN

A relationship between Wolf and Raven is not one made in heaven. Their personality traits and personal interests are not on the same plane. But both bring to this relationship a willingness to find common ground, which would make a coming together of emotions and intellect possible.

WOLF AND SERPENT

Connected through the element water, this is a case of two people who are capable of deep emotions. Most of all, they both are attracted to spiritual matters. It is a promising mixture of romance, which Wolf supplies, and passion, which Serpent offers. One can safely assume that this relationship will have a solid emotional as well as sexual foundation.

WOLF AND OWL

Wolf and Owl have much to give to each other. First, however, they need to overcome a few difficulties in communication. These difficulties are the

result of Wolf idealizing his dreams while Owl lives, works, and if necessary, fights for an ideal world. The key to understanding here is not in learning how to communicate but rather in acknowledging the nature of the differences. Search for resolution of these real but minor differences, if both pursue it, could enormously enrich this relationship.

WOLF AND GOOSE

A combination of water and earth could result in a very satisfying relationship. Both Wolf and Goose of course need to contribute to the success. The relationship requires more than compassion. Every now and then Goose should be less disciplined, and Wolf should delve into the depth of his dreams when Goose is able to join him.

WOLF AND OTTER

Wolf and Otter are not very compatible partners. But with a bit of goodwill, they should be able to find common ground. Wolf asks of Otter not only intellectual but also emotional openness. If Otter is able to make this leap, Wolf will find a partner the likes of which she only has imagined in her dreams. All Wolf has to do, every now and then, is make the journey from her head to her heart.

WOLF AND WOLF

Two Wolves together will reach an emotional depth that is difficult to put into words. In the depth of the water element, they will find dimensions and emotions that border on magic. Difficulty will only arise if both, in their rapture, lose sight of reality.

THE CYCLE OF
NATURE

‡‡‡

THE FALCON PERIOD

In Nature a Time of Awakening

Finally, winter has been conquered. Darkness must give way once more to light, which continuously increases in strength and duration. A sure sign of the approaching spring are the first buds that appear. With the warming air comes the promise that nature, and thereby life, is about to wake from its slumber. This moment of birth is full of dynamic power and optimism. To those who are born now belongs the world. No wonder—nature is brave and courageous, taking a chance on new beginnings. The adventure called life can begin and nothing and nobody will be able to stop it.

People, ideas, and projects conceived now will profit from the impetuous energy that is bursting toward the light of day as courageous as it is blind. In the truest sense, this means a breakthrough, which makes the Falcon period a time of confidence, spontaneity, and determination. What is needed now are pioneer spirit and courage, both of which could be the key to success. In other words, this is the perfect time to follow one's intuition and to begin new projects.

March 21–April 19

▼ ▼ ▼ ▼ ▼ ▼ ▼ ▼ ▼ ▼ ▼ ▼ ▼ ▼ ▼ ▼ ▼

Falcon is now in peak form because this is his time. **Salmon** and **Owl** can also have golden opportunities. **Deer** and **Otter** feel energized and motivated.

In Nature a Time of Growth

Now that new life has awakened in nature, small and still very sensitive leaves and blossoms are appearing with great expectations. The time is right to nurture what has been newly created. Nature is providing a safe and stable foundation that makes healthy growth possible. It becomes very apparent that the influence of the Sun, in northern climes, is growing stronger day by day. The days are getting longer and it is getting warmer. Not only plants but people also feel assured that there is no way to go but up. Such certainty provides confidence and strength.

People, ideas, and projects that are taking shape now are fundamentally positive but require a certain amount of levelheadedness. During the Beaver period it is important to stabilize what has been achieved so far, especially one's material and physical well-being. Just like Beaver himself, the period of the Beaver is a time of constructive creativity. Now is also the time to make long-term plans that require patience and sensible economic considerations.

April 20—May 20

▼▼▼▼▼▼▼▼▼▼▼▼▼▼▼▼

Beaver is now in peak form because this is his time. **Brown Bear** and **Goose** can have golden opportunities. **Woodpecker** and **Wolf** feel energized and motivated.

THE DEER PERIOD

In Nature a Time of Flowering

Nature awakened and created life with energy and strength in the Falcon period and developed roots and began to grow in the Beaver period. Now fragrant flowers begin to appear. Nature is producing a kaleidoscope of colors, and butterflies travel from one blossom to the next. Birds sing their songs with intense delight and enthusiasm. It is as if nature is having a great, big, wonderful feast, celebrating joyfully everything that surrounds us. Summer is not far away. Life can prosper. Nobody remains untouched. Everybody, it seems, would like the world to remain in this optimistic state.

People, ideas, and projects are taking shape. They mirror the many different facets and carefree outlook that make life during this period so joyful, happy, and promising. Contacts and connections are established; communication becomes the magic word for Deer and the Deer period. It is important to learn how things function and how they can be useful. Things that have to do with commerce, transportation, and education are particularly promising during this period.

May 21–June 20

▼ ▼ ▼ ▼ ▼ ▼ ▼ ▼ ▼ ▼ ▼ ▼ ▼ ▼ ▼ ▼

Deer is now in peak form because this is his time. **Raven** and **Otter** can also have golden opportunities. **Falcon** and **Salmon** feel energized and motivated.

THE WOODPECKER PERIOD

In Nature a Time for Concentration

With the South Wind, summer arrives. The days are long and the night gentle. Nature unfolds in all its splendor, even though the high point of the cycle passes with the summer solstice near June 21st. Days begin to grow shorter, though we are barely aware of it. Now nature concentrates on what it has created to assure continuity. This is the time of intense, strong emotions reciprocated with trust. After all, who would want to think of things being in decline when the season is at its zenith.

People, ideas, and projects that are taking shape right now are influenced by strong emotions. The Woodpecker period is the time when everything is deeply rooted in life. This is when close emotional bonds are formed. During this period it is not the head, but our inner feelings that rule our lives. Whatever is happening or being planned now must be accepted and carried first and foremost by our emotions. This is why we must avoid making important decisions on the spur of the moment.

June 21–July 21

▼ ▼ ▼ ▼ ▼ ▼ ▼ ▼ ▼ ▼ ▼ ▼ ▼ ▼ ▼ ▼

Woodpecker is in peak form because this is his time. **Serpent** and **Wolf** can also have golden opportunities. **Beaver** and **Brown Bear** feel energized and motivated.

THE SALMON PERIOD

In Nature a Time of Ripening

Nature seems to be more powerful than ever before. The heat of the summer spreads optimism, but it will also make us slightly lazy. Nature is full of energy, life shows us its most powerful, generous, and luxuriant side. Summer has reached its crescendo and gives no, or only small, hints of the coming fall. Only the fruit ripening in the trees tells us that the time of harvest and reflection is not too far away. But nobody wants to think about it. We would rather concentrate on relishing life as it is now. Nature gives itself away and people have no difficulty being emotionally open.

People, ideas, and projects taking shape right now will bounce with energy and experience a strong sense of self-worth and self-confidence. Courageous and formidable plans are made during the period of the Salmon, and they are going to succeed because people now have not only enthusiasm but ambition and determination as well. Life and nature are bursting with unbelievable riches, and people produce a wealth of ideas and projects. Whatever is started during the Salmon period will be of high quality, and it will succeed.

July 22–August 21

▼ ▼ ▼ ▼ ▼ ▼ ▼ ▼ ▼ ▼ ▼ ▼ ▼ ▼ ▼ ▼

Salmon is now in peak form because this is his time. **Falcon** and **Owl** can also have golden opportunities. **Deer** and **Raven** feel energized and motivated.

THE BROWN BEAR PERIOD

In Nature a Time of Harvest

Now summer is coming to an end. Nature's gifts are being harvested and stored. The days grow shorter, the Sun loses some of its intensity. Birds fly south, a sure sign that colder and darker days are ahead. Now is the time to prepare for the winter months to come. It is a time of diligent, unceasing work, but this is also a time for gratitude. Since the Falcon period, nature has propelled us forward, inspired us, and smiled on us. This is time for taking stock, to make good use of what we have been given. This is a time to discover our own inner qualities.

People, ideas, and projects that are taking shape right now are based on logic and usefulness. The Brown Bear period is a time for evaluating details more closely and for setting aside one's ego. Our responsibilities need to be recognized and put into practice. Again we must set aside our own needs for the greater good. In a broader sense, the Brown Bear period stands for modesty, economy, and service to others without neglecting oneself.

August 22–September 21

▼ ▼ ▼ ▼ ▼ ▼ ▼ ▼ ▼ ▼ ▼ ▼ ▼ ▼ ▼ ▼

Brown Bear is in peak form because this is his time. **Beaver** and **Goose** can also have golden opportunities. **Woodpecker** and **Serpent** feel energized and motivated.

THE RAVEN PERIOD

In Nature a Time of Retreat

Fall has arrived. The Sun is losing strength and darkness begins to grow. The nights are longer. Nature, giving tribute to the conclusion of the second cycle, puts on a display of spectacular colors—much as she did when everything was bursting into full bloom during the Deer period. In northern latitudes, before the leaves fall to the ground and nature withdraws to a more quiet phase, we can feast our eyes on the magical colors of the foliage. Migratory birds fly to warmer climes, and animals are preparing winter stocks and dens for hibernation. A strange quietness fills the air.

People, ideas, and projects that are taking shape right now are influenced by the need for balance, harmony, and fairness. The Raven period is a time to work with and to accept contradictions. This requires a deeper understanding for others or, at least, a good measure of diplomacy and compromise. This is not really a time to make important decisions. This is a time of evaluating, comparing, and preparing for decisions to be made down the road that will be fair for everybody and everything involved.

September 22–October 22

▼ ▼ ▼ ▼ ▼ ▼ ▼ ▼ ▼ ▼ ▼ ▼ ▼ ▼ ▼ ▼

Raven is in peak form because this is his time.
Deer and **Otter** can also have golden opportunities.
Salmon and **Owl** feel energized and motivated.

THE SERPENT PERIOD

In Nature a Time of Death and Transformation

Nature is going through the Serpent period. This includes the process of dying; the period of farewell hovers in the air. The Sun has lost much of its power, providing less energy for plants to remain alive. Once-colorful foliage now covers the ground. Strong winds are blowing down the last remaining leaves to form a protection for the Earth from the bitter cold that is to come. The process of dying is also a time of transformation, because decaying plants, turned into humus, provide the soil with nourishing food, making it possible for the natural cycle to produce new life.

People born during this period will challenge themselves; ideas and projects will be easy to realize. Part of the lesson to be learned during the Serpent period is to find out who or what becomes a thing of the past. The limits of physical and emotional obligations need to be determined because this is the time of transformation: a time of holding on and letting go, of keeping and discarding, of dying and rebirth. The big question, however, is how to use one's energies: constructively or destructively?

October 23–November 22
▼ ▼ ▼ ▼ ▼ ▼ ▼ ▼ ▼ ▼ ▼ ▼ ▼ ▼ ▼ ▼

Serpent is now in peak form because this is his time.
Woodpecker and **Wolf** can have golden opportunities.
Brown Bear and **Goose** feel energized and motivated.

121

THE OWL PERIOD

In Nature a Time of Hibernation

During the Owl period nature has fallen into a deep sleep. She is already dreaming about renewal, which makes this a time for hope and confidence. The Sun reaches the lowest point in the sky, the winter solstice. Every day now, depending on where you live, can consist of two-thirds darkness. Nature and people alike are sustained by the belief that these gloomy times will soon be transformed and that the light will return. Until then, nature is in a deep sleep, surrounding us with silence and anticipation that demands that we be more introspective and spiritual.

People, ideas, and projects being shaped now bring a spark to the world. The Owl period is the time of deeply rooted faith in the good—something that nourishes visions and new plans that are supported by enthusiasm and idealism. That's why it is very important to have strong convictions about what is planned—to believe that it is worth the effort. The goals that Owl people set for themselves are very ambitious and demanding, just like the plans made during this period. Much spontaneous and even euphoric energy is required to set things in motion; the most important thing is that everything we plan rests on a sound spiritual foundation.

November 23–December 21

▼ ▼ ▼ ▼ ▼ ▼ ▼ ▼ ▼ ▼ ▼ ▼ ▼ ▼ ▼ ▼ ▼

Owl is now in peak form because this is his time.
Falcon and **Salmon** can also have golden opportunities.
Raven and **Otter** feel energized and motivated.

In Nature a Time of Renewal

The Earth is covered with ice and snow; all life seems to be frozen. But through the ice and cold we get a sense of something immaculate as well as a readiness to break through the apparent paralysis. During the Goose period, nature sends definite signals of progress, first almost undetectably, then with increasing strength. While the Sun is still missing its penetrating power, days begin to get longer. The seed of hope, planted during the Owl period, begins to germinate and to take definite shape. Nature and people have accepted the challenge, and they will humbly and with increasing strength surpass themselves.

People, ideas, and projects that take shape now must prove that they can, with determination, rise to the occasion and that they will find the key to long-lasting success. The road, steadily rising, leads us from the deepest depth to the highest summit. That can be difficult and stressful. And it sometimes requires clear vision, realistic assessments and, most of all, a sensible and diligent use of resources. Plans made during the Goose period require a strong foundation that will support every step taken along the way to the goal.

December 22–January 19

▼ ▼ ▼ ▼ ▼ ▼ ▼ ▼ ▼ ▼ ▼ ▼ ▼ ▼ ▼ ▼

Goose is now in peak form because this is his time.
Beaver and **Brown Bear** can have golden opportunities.
Serpent and **Wolf** feel energized and motivated.

THE OTTER PERIOD

In Nature a Time of Preparation

Frost and snow have not yet disappeared. Winter is still showing its unforgiving side, and it seems winter will never end. But something is changing: it is the power of the Sun. Victoriously, it climbs higher and higher in the sky in northern climes; soon cold and darkness will have to yield to its powerful rays. Winter's silence is changing more and more to expectation and restlessness. We can already see tiny, tender buds that are waiting to grow and burst open as soon as nature gives the go-ahead. Moving toward the conclusion of the Otter period, the Sun begins to melt the ice, and every now and then we get a waft of spring.

People, ideas, and projects that are taking shape now are programmed for progress. Humanism and justice are the headlines of the Otter period. Eyes look to the future. Activities and goals are organized around the idea of reforming the world, and the resulting changes may have grave consequences. It is a time to analyze trends as well as tried-and-true methods, and if necessary, to reform them. This is a good time for radical changes and reorientation as well as for group and community projects that emphasize social and humanitarian principles.

January 20–February 18

▼ ▼ ▼ ▼ ▼ ▼ ▼ ▼ ▼ ▼ ▼ ▼ ▼ ▼ ▼ ▼

Otter is now in peak form because this is his time. **Deer** and **Raven** can also have golden opportunities. **Falcon** and **Owl** feel energized and motivated.

THE WOLF PERIOD

In Nature a Time of Rebirth

Hope and expectation begin to assume the face of certainty. With early hints of spring, a time for rebirth and new beginnings is imminent. While ice and snow still linger, winter bows to the increasing strength of the Sun. The first buds and courageous flowers announce the new life about to break through. The old cycle of nature is coming to an end, and a new cycle is about to begin.

People, ideas, and projects that are taking shape now are filled with new hope, devotion, and a more or less conscious faith in the natural world. This extends to things, situations, and people. During the Wolf period, concepts like service to your fellow humans are not simply romantic notions or empty words but, rather, the content and foundation of all that we think and do. For that reason, projects and activities are based on loving intentions and selfless thoughts. Instinct and intuition are now the best counsel. However, beware the danger that people's generosity and trust may be exploited.

February 19–March 20

▼ ▼ ▼ ▼ ▼ ▼ ▼ ▼ ▼ ▼ ▼ ▼ ▼ ▼ ▼ ▼

Wolf is now in peak form because this is his time.
Woodpecker and **Serpent** have golden opportunities.
Beaver and **Goose** feel energized and motivated.

Mother Earth

What separates Native American culture from the Western World is the way Native Americans—the First Peoples of North and South America—understand nature and how they treat it. According to their understanding, people and the Earth are one. In addition, Earth is the Mother of all peoples, animals, and every form of life that has made Earth home. Native American people do not feel, as many Westerners do, that they are surrounded by a hostile environment. On the contrary, they feel protected and secure because of the never-ending care of the Great Mother.

The Blackfeet express it this way: "The Earth loves us, she is happy when she hears us sing. She provides the nourishment we need."

A tribe in Western Canada called the Thaltan express a similar sentiment: "The Earth is alive, she is our mother, because if she did not exist neither would we. The people are her children as are the animals. The stones are her bones, the water her milk, the animals are the same as people; they are from the same blood; they are related."

Index